THE
ASSESSMENT
OF
EARLY CHILD
DEVELOPMENT

THE
ASSESSMENT
OF
EARLY CHILD
DEVELOPMENT

DOROTHY FLAPAN, Ph.D.
and
PETER B. NEUBAUER, M.D.

JASON ARONSON INC.
Northvale, New Jersey
London

THE MASTER WORK SERIES

First softcover edition 1994

Copyright © 1983, 1979, 1975 by Jason Aronson Inc.

ISBN: 1-56821-284-4
Library of Congress Catalog Number: 84-0450013

Manufactured in the United States of America. Jason Aronson Inc. offers books and cassettes. For information and catalog write to Jason Aronson Inc., 230 Livingston Street, Northvale, New Jersey 07647.

Contents

Preface

Interest in early child development has expanded rapidly as the importance of these early years has become increasingly recognized and as the identification in infancy of children at risk and those with developmental disorders and vulnerabilities has become possible. Knowledge of child development and pathology is invaluable to everyone involved with children: child-care workers, physicians, psychiatrists, psychologists, nurses, public-health workers, teachers, social workers, family-life educators, and others.

It is not surprising that people from such a diversity of fields and backgrounds would have diverse approaches to the assessment of child development. As a consequence, however, they encounter difficulties in communicating with one another and problems in comparing research findings. Therefore, there is both a need and a demand for a more unified approach to the understanding of child development and for standard procedures for assessing the development of young children.

This book is an attempt to meet that need. The overview of early development and the format of its presentation—with developmental charts that summarize aspects of development in a graphic way and a short assessment outline, which can be used for individual children—evolved as we reported our initial formulations and findings from several subsequent research projects at meetings, conferences, and workshops with colleagues and paraprofessionals working with children. These sessions included the following: the Annual Interdepartmental Meeting of the staff of the Jewish Board of Guardians; a seminar of the Sociology Department at Hunter College of the City of New York; a conference at the Washington Square Institute for Psychotherapy and Mental Health; a workshop for graduate students in Special Education at Hunter College; staff meetings at the Child Development Center; and various professional meetings of psychologists, psychiatrists, and psychoanalysts. On all of these occasions we received helpful comments, questions, and criticisms, which led us to clarify our formulations about the various aspects of development.

The Short Assessment Outline was derived from the research studies of young children conducted over many years, in which parents and nursery-school, kindergarten, and primary-grade teachers participated. The Downtown Community School was the first to cooperate with us in the study of children attending their nursery school. Hartley House, Hudson Guild, and the Bloomingdale Project also participated by making their nursery schools available to us. Throughout the early development of the Short Assessment Outline, the staff and teachers of these schools helped with suggestions to make it more practical and easier to use.

Improved versions of the Short Assessment Outline were then tried in some New York City public schools, as well as by nursery-school teachers and pediatricians at the Child Development Center. We incorporated the comments and suggestions they offered during these trials, and we would like to express our appreciation to them and to thank them for their contributions.

Most of all we would like to thank the officers of the Grant Foundation, who generously supported this study from the beginning. They encouraged us first to undertake the initial systematic study of early child development and then to assess the children from different socioeconomic groups in order to compare these findings with those obtained from our earlier investigation. They demonstrated much interest throughout our studies. This book is the final product of the longitudinal comparative studies of children.

On the basis of our various presentations and the reactions we have received from colleagues and paraprofessionals, we have some assurance that people from many different fields, with quite different backgrounds, have been able to use the Short Assessment Outline for their diversified purposes in different settings. We hope, therefore, that this book will make a contribution toward a more unified approach to the early assessment of children.

Dorothy Flapan, Ph.D.
Peter Neubauer, M.D.

Chapter 1
Need for a Short
Assessment Outline

Theory and recent research have alerted professionals and nonprofessionals to the importance of the early years of childhood; and during the past several years the number of professionals and paraprofessionals in the fields of day-care, early childhood education, pediatrics, and community health has increased greatly.

Throughout the United States, programs in the areas of physical and mental health and education have been and are being developed to investigate the wide variety of services that could be offered for children, beginning in infancy and continuing through adolescence. Existing services are being expanded to reach more children than ever before, children ranging from the normal to the abnormal and from many diverse socioeconomic and sociocultural backgrounds.

Cognitive development has been especially emphasized because many children have shown difficulties in their learning capacities. Programs have been instituted to teach children basic mathematical and scientific concepts as early as at the nursery-school and kindergarten levels. Techniques have been developed to improve reading readiness, to increase vocabulary, and to teach the use of symbols and approaches to solve complicated intellectual problems, thereby improving performances on standard intelligence tests. Much effort has gone also into devising methods to arouse the children's curiosity and to motivate them, in order to encourage them to learn.

It is necessary, however, for those who are in regular contact with young children to broaden their perspectives and to take responsibility for more than the support of cognitive development if they are to contribute to a fuller realization of the children's potentialities. Many young children have anxieties and unresolved conflicts that are beyond the usual expected developmental problems and that interfere with their current functioning and their further development. Serious pathology in the first years of life may slow or distort development. In fact, it has been found that some children entering nursery-school are already so limited by their earlier experiences that they are unable to respond to, or benefit from, the environment provided within the schoolroom, so that "learning" does not take place unless special conditions are made available. Consequently, much interest has been expressed in being able to recognize and evaluate the problems and difficulties of children in the early stages.

It is our conviction that it is necessary for those who work with children to know the major aspects of development and to be able to assess these. Such knowledge would then enable them to set up more appropriate programs within schools, clinics, and child guidance agencies.

It is also important that those who are in contact with children know what is within the variation of normality in development and the indices that development may be outside this range. We assume, of course, that as part of their normal development children go through periods of conflict, that there is considerable variability within the wide range of normality in development, and that at times children who are developing normally may experience problems and difficulties beyond the norm.

Those in ongoing in-service programs for nursery-school teachers, day-care workers, pediatricians, and community health specialists, as well as those in innovative educational programs at community colleges and graduate schools, have for some time voiced a need for an outline that would systematically present "expectable developmental progression." Such an outline would be even more valuable if it could be used as a reliable initial "screening device" and as an aid in deciding on the type of assistance needed for a specific child, be it a referral to a clinic, a one-to-one relationship with a "special" adult, or a contribution by various means to improving ego skills.

Day-care centers, public-health agencies, community health programs, social agencies, and pediatric services are channels for early contact and interaction with children. Professional and paraprofessional staff in these settings are in a crucial position to assess, "screen," and differentiate between children with serious pathology who need treatment, children who need emotional support, and children who need only some modifications in their environment, such as minimizing the stresses and strains that might contribute to problems or offering additional services or special attention. Experiences that build on a child's strengths may be provided and experiences that contribute further to a child's current problems or create additional difficulties for him may be eliminated or delayed for a while. Those who are in regular contact with the child may aid him in establishing relationships with peers and with adults other than his parents, or they may encourage him to express and assert himself and to "try himself out" in new situations.

Beyond their direct, daily work with the child and his parents, professionals and paraprofessionals can make an important contribution by becoming sensitized to a child's showing signs of developing more serious problems and signs of conflict and anxiety, so that the child who needs it will receive the required help at as early an age as possible. They may use the services of psychiatric consultants, psychologists, and social workers—designating some children for further intensive study and evaluation or referring others to a mental health resource in the community for therapeutic help directly or through supportive work with parents.

There are, then, two tasks involved: (1) to become aware of the various forms of behavior which have to be observed in order to assess the development of children and (2) to communicate the observations in the standardized, systematic form to colleagues and consultants. Thus, an assessment outline is desirable as a tool to determine where each child is in his ongoing development and as a means of transmitting information to others. Used periodically throughout the year and over a number of years, such an assessment outline would assist professionals and paraprofessionals to follow a child's developmental progression and to determine how each child in his own individual way passes through the developmental stages. It would also contribute toward planning in the natural settings of the child conditions which can assist him in coping with the expected developmental conflicts and problems or toward planning the types of outside services that would be helpful.

There are many developmental outlines and developmental profiles available which attempt to be comprehensive by taking in as many areas and variables as possible and integrating these in order to achieve a complete clinical assessment of the child. However, such a thorough profile takes a great deal of knowledge about children's development and a great deal of clinical training before it can be used validly. Also, much time is required to prepare such a full developmental assessment of a child. Thus, this type of assessment or profile is limited in its use and could not be followed easily by the nonclinical professionals and paraprofessionals who are most urgently in need of assessment instruments today.

Researchers have also made some effort to develop rating forms which range from problem checklists to traits and personality-structure assessment. Although these can be filled out in a relatively short time, most of them assess only pathological behavior or concentrate on cognitive development and do not give an integrated overview of the child's development.

With the obvious need in mind, the Child Development Center of the Jewish Board of Guardians began a long-term research project, with this goal: to produce a valid, reliable, short assessment instrument that could be used by clinical and nonclinical professionals, as well as by paraprofessionals, to observe the development of children during their early years.

Chapter 2
Study of Early
Child Development

Research was designed with the aim of systematically studying early child development so that an outline would evolve. This outline would emphasize a few essential features of development, rather than being an extensive, complete assessment, and would permit a preliminary grouping of children. Only the minimum necessary information was to be included. In this way, gross judgments could be made about the children; and from an initial assessment an overall sketch of each child's development could be obtained, which could be the basis for planning for that child. This initial "screening" also could lead to further intensive study whenever it was deemed advisable.

The Child Development Center was in a favorable position to work on the task of evolving an assessment instrument that would be acceptable to, and usable by, a variety of groups of clinical and nonclinical staff. It had available a staff of clinicians with many years of experience both in diagnosing young children with various difficulties and in providing a variety of modalities of help through a therapeutic nursery school, an outpatient clinic for young children and their parents, group counseling programs with mothers, and consultation arrangements with various neighborhood schools and agencies.

An additional factor was the Child Development Center's long tradition of an interprofessional approach—psychiatrists, psychologists, social workers, and teachers working together to bring many different perspectives to bear on the task.

The ultimate goal of our research was to use clinical knowledge and experience in a way that could make a contribution to those who were in regular daily contact with young children, to bridge the separation between clinicians and nonclinicians so that the fruits of clinical experience could be carried over to the larger community.

At the beginning of our study, we conceptualized assessment in terms of the child's mental health and sought to define mental health in such a way as to provide the basis of assessment. A review of the relevant literature indicated various ways in which health was defined.

1. In one approach, "health" was equated with "normality," which was based on a statistical "average" or norm. Each individual child would then be compared with this standard. However, this accepted the status quo and implied that what is found in the society is normal and therefore healthy. It also suggested an adaptation to the existing society, a "fitting in." Yet what is the norm or "healthy" in one society is not necessarily the norm in another and therefore not regarded as healthy in the other society.

2. Another approach in the literature defined health in terms of the absence of pathology. In many instances, it is easier to diagnose pathology than health and thus to define health as a double negative—no pathology. However, it is important to look also at a child's positive strengths. The absence of a negative condition does not satisfactorily assess positive factors. In addition, what looks like pathology in children may not necessarily be pathology but may rather be part of the normal developmental progress, and the alternation of progression and regression are an expected part of the normal developmental trend. Also, the absence of surface symptoms may not be significant, since children may function well while suffering underlying conflict.

3. A third approach in the literature was to define health as an optimal or ideal condition. It was then this optimal condition against which each individual child was assessed. There is a problem here of defining the variables and criteria to use in setting up a health ideal. As these in turn depend on one's theoretical orientation, it is difficult to get "experts" to agree on what the ideal health condition is.

Definitions such as these create additional problems when one attempts to set forth criteria of health and to measure it, or when one tries to determine the criteria of pathology and the interrelationships between health and pathology. Our first paper spelled out in detail our thoughts on this problem.[1]

In view of the factors just mentioned and the influence of Anna Freud, we shifted our approach. Instead of attempting to assess health or pathology, we decided to focus on understanding developmental progression. With such an approach, we were no longer primarily concerned with diagnostic statements of pathology but rather tried to discover to what degree and in what form pathology interfered with developmental progression.

After an exploratory study of a sample of nursery-school children and after many months devoted to seminars, workshops, and discussions of this problem, we decided that we should indeed consider as the major task of childhood the capacity to maintain development. We would use, as a yardstick by which to assess children and to differentiate among them, those criteria which indicate the normal, "expectable" progression in development. (Here, too, we faced the problem of agreeing on what we considered to be normal development, taking into account the individual variations and the differences between boys and girls.)

At the time we began our study, this was a novel approach in evaluating children, but one which we thought had several positive aspects. In the judgment of our research staff, "developmental progression" can be more easily defined and agreed upon than can "health' or "normality," and thus the developmental approach seemed to offer better potential for establishing validity and reliability. Also, it was our judgment that the developmental consideration would be more useful to both clinicians and nonclinicians.

We preferred the developmental approach also for another reason: Health as a "state of being" is assessed at one moment in time, whereas development, being ongoing and continuous and with change as its central aspect, is evaluated over a period of time. Since development may proceed in spurts and stops, and periodic

1. See Dorothy Flapan and Peter B. Neubauer, "Issues in Assessing Development," *Journal of the American Academy of Child Psychiatry* 9: 669-687, 1970.

regression may be followed by progression, a cross-sectional assessment of health will give an inaccurate picture of the child. What at one cross-sectional assessment would be judged as either abnormal or normal might change in subsequent assessments. Assessments at a given moment may give a misleading picture of health, since what is seen as malfunctioning may be corrected by a process of change over a period of time. On the other hand, what is seen at a given moment as unhealthy may, in the long run, be of little significance for the child. Thus, some disorders may appear to have much significance in terms of a child's current functioning but may have little significance in long-range terms. Also, an assessment at a given moment of time may be misleading since latent developmental difficulties cannot be observed. The developmental approach takes into account changes over time and thus builds into the design the changing conditions of the child's developmental process.

Developmental assessment does not try to make a statement according to some diagnosis based on a symptom evaluation alone. Its aim is to determine whether disorders or symptoms have interfered with further development and how the processes of development in turn have affected the symptoms of children. This mode of assessment differs from field-oriented and field-specific diagnostic categories because it takes into account the moving and changing characteristics of children. In children we find frequent changes of symptoms, and in different children the same changes of symptoms have different meanings. Also, there may be a change of symptoms without a change in the underlying conflict. When we look only at pathology at a cross-sectional level, we cannot be sure about the effect of pathology on development.

Formulation of the Research

When the research study was originally formulated at the Child Development Center, we set forth a plan involving four steps. First, we were to apply the methods of studying children in a clinical setting to a sample of nonclinical children who were attending nursery schools in the community. In this initial phase of the study, we set up an Outline Guide that would result in as comprehensive and complete an assessment of each child as clinically possible.

Second, we were to follow this nonclinical population over a period of several years, wtih annual assessment of each child, to discover which children developed serious problems or disturbances and the types of problems. Our focus was to be primarily on the children. In this study we did not plan to examine the parents' influence on the children's development.

Third, we were to carry out a detailed analysis of the areas of development and those aspects of behavior of the children which permitted us to differentiate between various groups of children.

Fourth, we intended to reduce the more complete outline to a shorter one that would incorporate the essential features. This short form could then be made available for use by people in direct contact with young children—psychologists, psychiatrists, social workers, nursery-school teachers, public-health nurses, pediatricians, child-care workers, and community health workers.

Data Gathering

The research project began with the study of a large sample of middle-class children attending a private nursery school in the community, one at which the parents paid a moderate tuition. All the parents were college graduates and many had graduate degrees. These fathers and mothers were mainly in professions such as law, medicine, engineering, and the arts, or they were business executives. Later, the study was extended to include samples of working-class children who were on scholarships in private nursery schools or were in nursery schools in various community centers or settlement houses. Almost all the parents of these children were high-school graduates but had no college education. They were mainly policemen, firemen, bus drivers, postal workers, and blue-collar workers.

In all the samples of children, those who were judged to be retarded, schizophrenic, or organically brain damaged and those who were currently receiving psychotherapy, were excluded. Thus, the study had a select group of "average" children, considered by their parents and their teachers to be functioning more or less adequately at home and in the nursery school.

These children were seen initially when they were three-four years of age, then at four-five, and finally at five-six.

The usual clinical method of data gathering was followed. This included semistructured interviews with each of the children, their parents, and their teachers; observations of the children in the school setting; and administration of a battery of psychological tests. The interviews and observations were undertaken by psychiatrists, psychologists, and psychiatric social workers, all of whom followed an extensive interview guide based on psychoanalytic assumptions.[2] In addition, psychological examiners administered the Stanford Binet Intelligence Test, the Rorschach ink blots, the Children's Apperception Tests, and a figure-drawing test.[3]

The clinician who did the interviewing and observing made an assessment of the child's development on the basis of each source of information. The psychological examiner made an assessment of the child's developmental status based on the psychological tests administered. Then, the clinician wrote a summary integrating the material from all the interviews and observations with the information from the psychological tests. A final assessment of the child's developmental status, based on the integration of all the information available, was then made by the clinical staff. (Such complete data gathering and assessment required about twenty-five hours each year for each child.)

Groupings of the Children

This complete workup of clinical material was used as a basis for differentiating between groups of children. After several different

---

2. Interviewers included: R. Barazani, Ph.D.; B. Cramer, M.D.; L. Dimitrovsky, Ph.D.; D. Flapan, Ph.D.; N. Frankel, M.D.; L. Friedberger, Ph.D.; T. Gardian, M.S.W.; R. Geller, Ph.D.; G. Gunn, M.A.; P. Gunther, M.A.; J. Hart, M.A.; J. Kuppersmith, Ph.D.; H. Rahtz, M.S.W.; L. Sabot, M.D.; A. Sax, M.D.; M. Stein, M.D.; A. Tucker, Ph.D.

3. Psychological examiners included: S. Farber, Ph.D.; L. Friedberger, Ph.D.; L. Gruenthal; J. Kuppersmith, Ph.D.; A. Tucker, Ph.D.

ways of grouping, the children were tested, the following groupings finally evolved.[4]

Group 1. Progression in development has been maintained
   a. Without accompanying pathology.
   b. With significant accompanying pathological features.

Group 2. Progression in development has been interfered with in significant areas.

Group 3. Progression in development *had* been interfered with in significant areas but is again proceeding.

The groupings were, therefore, organized around developmental process, and the primary task was to see which children followed the normal pattern of development, which had difficulties but continued with their development and which fell outside the range of normal development.[5]

When we tested these groupings, we found that it was possible for us to differentiate between the four groupings of children and to achieve agreement among trained clinicians in assessing the children. In other words, it was possible (1) to differentiate between children who maintained development and those who showed interference with development in significant areas and (2) to differentiate between children with significant pathology and those with minimal pathology.[6]

4. These findings appear in Dorothy Flapan and Peter B. Neubauer, "Developmental Groupings of Pre-School Children," *The Israel Annals of Psychiatry and Related Disciplines* 10: 52-70, 1972.

5. It should be noted that the difference between Group 1a and Group 1b is not equal to that between Group 2 and Group 3. These are not groups differentiated quantitatively but rather differentiated qualitatively. The numbers permit the setting up of different groups, which could easily be designed A^1, A^2, B and C, instead of 1a, 1b, 2, and 3.

6. Dorothy Flapan and Peter B. Neubauer, "Developmental Groupings of Pre-School Children," *The Israel Annals of Psychiatry and Related Disciplines* 10: 52-70, 1972.

Aspects of Development

In order to assess developmental progression in young children, it was important to decide which aspects of development were most significant. Several preliminary questions had to be answered before systematic data gathering was started. Specifically, *what* was to be evaluated? *How* was it to be evaluated? *Which* general areas of development and specific behaviors within each area were to be examined? How feasible was it to obtain the desired information?

To arrive at the final Short Assessment Outline, it was necessary to use a long form first and then to reduce it. There was a continuous reduction over many years of data gathering (see Appendix A). The final form was based on the years of research with children and of experimenting with different formats. Some of the items on this form are similar to items in other ratings or checklists. However, the integration of all items into one overall picture reflects our own experience.

A developmental approach, looking at many developmental lines at the same time, had been discussed for some time by Anna Freud. She emphasized the assessment of all aspects of development rather than just one isolated aspect. Our work was greatly influenced by Miss Freud, as well as by other writers.[7]

Based on a theoretical model derived from psychoanalytic developmental psychology, it was assumed that development proceeds in stages. At each phase, the child is expected to show certain developmental and maturational landmarks and phase specific organization, with certain anxieties and conflicts. In his social milieu, the child encounters expectations and conditions with which he must cope at each stage. He has experience which may affect his development and exhibits characteristics, skills, and behaviors which can be taken as indices of his developmental progression.

We found in this research study that the staff (as well as the teachers) tended to evaluate the children in terms of their "own" spontaneous guidelines. Over the several years of the study, the

---

7. Such writers as E. H. Erikson, L. B. Murphy, M. Mahler, J. W. Macfarlane, S. Chess, and A. Thomas.

child's relationships with others usually were mentioned first and most frequently in assessing a child's developmental progression, although the child's affect, or "mood" was also heavily emphasized and frequently referred to. It appeared in this sample of nonclinical children, that anxieties, concerns and problems were most likely to show up in the child's relationships with others.[8] Thus the social development of children was selected as a primary dimension for the assessment of developmental progression. However, if the child gave the impression of being predominantly "happy" or "sad," this also strongly influenced the evaluation. Therefore, emotional development was considered another essential aspect of development to be assessed. Since social development and emotional development were given such significance by our research staff in making their evaluations of the children, these two aspects of development are presented in the next two chapters, before other aspects of development.

Because the study was based on a psychoanalytic developmental framework, we considered it also important to look at ego development, phase development (which includes the libidinal phases of development and the aggressive drive), and superego development (which includes self-esteem and the ego-ideal). Each of these areas of development has an important role in the overall assessment of the child's developmental progression, and we therefore devote a chapter to each.

Our interest was focused more on general developmental progression than on criteria for specific age-norms for a given item. For that reason we attempted to state in broad general terms the expected development within each given area and then selected items for which there were overt behavioral references. This meant translating theoretical concepts and propositions into observable behaviors from which inferences could be made—that is, describing specific forms of behavior that would be included within each area.

8. Often, even though a child was experiencing various conflicts or difficulties that affected developmental progression, he could continue functioning intellectually in the school situation and could more or less maintain the same I.Q. when tested.

In addition to making inferences from observed behavior, we also considered it necessary to look at absences of behaviors, traits, and trends usually expected and taken for granted as part of the developmental progression. In summary, we assumed that information about various activities, traits, and symptoms, would make it possible to draw inferences or generalizations about developmental progression within a given aspect of development; and from these inferences and generalizations, an assessment of overall progression and of pathology could be made.

Chapter 3
Social Development

We can assess a child's progression in social development by observing the persons to whom the child characteristically relates and the ways in which he relates to them. We expect that as he matures he will form relationships with more and more persons and that there will be a differentiation in the quality of these relationships. In addition, we look for an increasing interest in the needs of others and an increasing sensitivity to their reactions.

Separation-Individuation

Separation refers to the capacity of the child to distance himself from the mother, and *individuation* refers to his evolvement of self, his entity as an "I," his individuality which permits increasing independence. Dr. Margaret Mahler has contributed the essential data on this aspect of development, based on her studies of the processes and steps of separation and individuation.

Separation is accompanied by the establishment of object-constancy. We mean by this that the child has "incorporated" mother and father sufficiently so that they have become a part of him, and he therefore no longer needs their geographic presence. With this incorporation, which then becomes structured within the child's own psychic system, he is able to leave his parents and to permit his parents to leave him. This ability to separate is an important indication of the normal developmental progression through which the child passes and is related to the expansion of the child's social interest. However, this aspect of development must be considered in reference to the overall development of the child, including the libidinal phase organization, the aggressive expressions, and other aspects to be discussed in subsequent chapters.

Indices of the child's capacity to separate include such items as the feelings aroused in him by his mother's absence for a short period of time; the ability to visit relatives and peers, at first for a short time and eventually for longer periods and even overnight; and the ability to attend nursery school regularly. Intense separation anxiety in any of these situations over an extended period of time would raise questions about the child's developmental progression and would be taken as a symptom to be investigated further.

Expanding Social Relations

Development moves from not differentiating between persons to a recognition of and response to familiar persons in his immediate environment. The child's first relationship is with the mothering person. However, soon thereafter he forms relationships with other family members and significant persons within the household. Tentatively he then experiments with relationships with peers. And ultimately he is able to relate to groups and socializing institutions in the community.

The child begins by developing a significant relationship with one person—the mothering person—and later establishes significant relationships with other members of the family. Here we are not referring to transient people in his life but rather to those who play an important role in his development. We assume that progression and maturation permit the child to expand his social experiences so that more and more people are of relative significance to him. This requires that there be differentiation of people, that the child "know" in some way the characteristics of each person with whom he relates. Consequently, there may also be different types of relating with different people. In other words, as the number of people with whom the child will interact increases, so do the qualitative differentiating components. Although in the beginning, members of the family (especially mother, father, and siblings) are of greatest significance, playmates become increasingly important from about ages three-four years old on. The emerging capacity of the child to form other relationships is based on the interplay with the primary person.

At first the infant perceives others as "things," not as persons. Soon, however, he is staring at those around him, is studying their faces, and is reaching out and touching them. He responds to their sounds and makes his own sounds; he observes their smiles and may smile in return. He grunts or makes movements to get the attention of those nearby and tries in his own ways to make contact. Gradually, he learns to imitate others—to wave, to hug, to kiss— and enjoys the responses these actions bring. When left alone in a room, he may express his objection with noises or cries; when he awakes from sleep, he may "call out" to bring the caretaking person to him. As he is able to maneuver around, he may follow this person and make demands of her. He may even begin to test out various behaviors to see which are approved and which are disapproved.

During the period of infancy, there may be recognition of father and some responsiveness to him. Later, the toddler may enjoy being with father and playing with him.

Early in his life, the child differentiates between adults and children and responds to them differently, seeming especially to "enjoy" the unique types of relating with children.

He shows interest in watching the activities of others. At the same time, he may begin to impose himself on them and try to affect their behaviors. He may engage in games of giving and taking back, of feeding and being fed. He tries to tell others what to do, scolds them, opposes them, and attempts to communicate his own preferences and dislikes.

In the differentiating (or phallic) phase, the child's developing awareness of his or her own sex identity will affect his interaction with others. Then, in the phase of family integration (or oedipal phase) the boy may be expected to become more competitive with father, especially for mother's favors, and at the same time will identify with father, whereas the girl in this phase is expected to be more seductive with father while identifying with mother and competing for father's attention. Regardless of sex, the oedipal child may try to play the parents against each other and to separate them.

When the young child enters nursery school he may, at first, relate to the teacher as though she were a mother-substitute and depend on her to satisfy his needs. He may expect the teacher to take care of him as mother had done and to show him similar affection. Later, however, he may show negativism with the teacher, argumentativeness, and a struggle for control. Eventually the child may start to identify with the teacher and try to copy her behaviors and endeavor by various actions to get her admiration and praise. At the same time, the developing awareness of his sex identity may also enter into his ways of relating to the teacher. By the time children reach kindergarten, however, they usually are friendly and cooperative and accept the teacher in her own unique role.

In addition to the adults, the child will also form significant relationships with siblings, peers, and other children, who may be younger or older than he. As an infant, he learned to recognize his siblings (as noted previously) and may have had some contacts with them and some interest in their activities, although his main concern and focus was mother. He may at times, as a toddler, try to imitate his siblings' gestures and behaviors. He wants to play with them and with other children and wants to play with their toys, even though he may not yet be ready to have them play with his. Gradually, he learns to participate in shared play with other children, including siblings, and to take turns. He competes with his siblings for the parents' attention and affection, as well as for toys and other material objects; at the same time he may show a "mothering" attitude toward a younger child in the family.

Children at nursery school and in the neighborhood become increasingly important, and some initial forms of friendship will be established. The capacity to ally himself with a child outside of the family will permit him to experiment in a different setting, one in which rivalry or competition may not be so pronounced as in his own family. Although in his earlier years the child may have noticed other children, his interest in them was only for short periods of time. By nursery-school age, parallel play with other children is typical—doing the same activities as another child and being next to him, but actually playing alone. At times he may show interest, however, in the ongoing activities of a child nearby or a small group of children in the room. Gradually he becomes able to participate in play with these other children and able to assert himself with them or to compete with them for equipment, toys, and attention. He may even spend some time with one child who is a special friend—but friendships, as well as enmities, at this period are unstable.

In time, the child learns to be a participant in cooperative play with one other child or with a small group of children. He becomes able to share his possessions or the attention of an adult, although at times this alternates with his being rivalrous with other children. He differentiates between other children and is consciously aware of who is absent and who is present each day at school. His interest in, and capacity for, group participation is developing; and he may even be the one to suggest taking turns with the equipment or materials. He is learning to function in a small-group situation.

During this phase, children do things in "bunches," such as crowding on the monkey bars or running in circles. They may make approaches to each other either directly or indirectly through toys and materials. In the group situation, they participate actively, offering ideas and responding to others in the group.

The peer group gains more and more importance to children in this phase of development. They are able to play simple group games and may try to join others who are already in the midst of a game or may try to be included in some other ongoing group activity. They learn to "joke" with one another and to show affection to one another. They "take roles" and "pretend" with one another. It becomes apparent, however, that each child has some knowledge about his own social standing within the group. Some children may express a liking for play with children of the same sex and same age as themselves, though some prefer the opposite sex; others will indiscriminately accept either sex and any age.

It can be seen from the preceding discussion that as we study the extent to which a child is able to relate to persons within and outside the family we can approach an assessment of his social developmental status. Inferences can be made as to how exclusive the child's relationship is to his mother and to other family members and as to his capacity to relate to teachers, peers, and others in his environment.

Quality of Relationships

The child not only relates to more and more persons as he matures and develops, but the quality of his social relationships also changes—from viewing the "other" only as an instrument for the satisfaction of his own needs to the eventual development of mutually satisfying, intimate, and long-lasting friendships. Thus, the forms and intensity of his relationships with others give an indication of the child's current level of social development. For example, a young child may appear to be able to relate mostly in a clinging, overdependent way or may appear to be able to have only transient, superficial relationships.

At the child's earliest age, the "other" exists primarily for his satisfaction and the "other" is expected to know and to meet the child's wishes and needs immediately and without conscious effort or communication on the part of the child. He experiences his mother (or mother surrogate) as indispensable for need gratification (food, help, play) and for comfort. The child demands immediate gratification and protection and often shows a need for intense body contact, with tendencies to "melt" with the other. Because he needs mother's presence and support, he tries to please her and later tries to get her approval. Abnormal relationships may be characterized by passivity, lack of initiative, and excessive reliance on the "other" (for dressing, toileting, and other tasks). Helplessness is an expression of the lack of independence, an invitation for mother to do everything for the child.

As he becomes aware of himself as separate from others, the child may try to control them in order not to be controlled by them. There may be frequent conflict with them and angry interaction. The child may be negativistic, dominating, or bossy in his relationships. At the same time, however, he may begin to show fear of reprimand and of punishment.

Following this phase, relationships may be competitive. The child may be exhibitionistic, attention-seeking, challenging, and rivalrous. And at a later period he may be characteristically manipulative, coy, and flirtatious in his relationships.

The child will learn from others about his own way of looking at things and feeling about them. Thus, the social expansion, in the sense in which we discuss it in this chapter, is based on processes of imitation, identification, and shifting and changing interaction systems that slowly build his own sense of "self" within the child.

Based on psychoanalytic developmental psychology, it is expected that each child will pass through several stages during his preschool and kindergarten years (see chapter 6, "Phase Development"). It is possible to assess his social development in reference to the needs satisfied in the social relationships (such as needs for contact, attention, approval, help, admiration, competition), the expectations and wishes, and the techniques used in relationships (such as demanding, whining, bossing, seducing)—to discover the motivations for behavior. It is also possible to look at the appropriateness of the child's social behaviors, especially with peers, and to look at his competence in approaching others, initiating contacts, and responding to the overtures of others.

Concern for Others

The social component of development also includes the child's empathy—that is, his ability to recognize individual ways others have of perceiving the world, reacting to it, and expressing themselves. To the degree that the child becomes able to differentiate within himself a variety of reactions and motives, he would be expected also to be able to recognize similar reactions and motives of others. Therefore, an ever-increasing quality of consideration for others can be anticipated. This may fluctuate at different times and in different situations. For example, in circumstances where the child feels tired or deprived, he may regress to earlier phases of life when he was more self-involved, whereas under other circumstances the demonstration of consideration for others may be higher. However, together with an increasing differentiation of himself and his relationships with others, we would look for an increasing capacity to be considerate. We would expect the child to become able to cooperate with others and to accept the concept of "being fair."

As he matures, it is also to be expected that he will show concern for the well-being of others, compassion, and an increasing capacity to share with others and to adapt to some extent to their needs. And we would expect indications of a developing sensitivity to others' moods and feelings—to know when another person (child or adult) feels hurt, feels angry or feels his rights have been violated. (This is discussed further in chapter 4, "Emotional Development.") Thus, in assessing the child's social development, it is important to look for evidences of the interest the child shows in the needs and reactions of others, his sensitivity to them, and his concern for them.

Impact on Others

As another essential area of social development, we want to assess the child's developing impact on his social environment—the responses of others to him. *Who* responds to him and *how* do they respond? Who ignores him and why? We can observe him in one-to-one relationships and in his participation as a group member in order to see his effect on others and on their activities.

In observing the social behavior of others (adults and children) in response to the child's behaviors, we can ask the following questions. How does he influence others? What is the general reaction to him as a person? Is he liked? Is he isolated? Is he criticized? Does he provoke angry feelings in others? Does he become the "victim"? Is he a child who is easily responded to with a sense of acceptance and friendliness? Or is he accepted with wariness and guardedness?

Observational data, as well as information from parents and teachers, enabled us to get some general clues about the impact the child had on other children and on adults. Thus, it was possible to assess him not only from the point of view of his own internal psychic function but also from an external viewpoint.

Assessment of Social Development

The information concerning the social aspects of development was easy for our research staff to obtain. Parents gave us information about the social functioning of the child, and teachers often spontaneously commented on the child's relationships with other children and with teachers, either in their written progress reports at the school or verbally in interviews with our staff. Social development is easily observable, particularly the ways in which the child approaches or reacts to his classmates and teachers, his parents, other family members, and other persons in his environment. Others' responses are also easily observable. Thus, it does not make an unreasonable demand on individuals who are in regular contact with the child to include this aspect of development in a short assessment outline. Yet such information is significant in assessing the child's developmental status.

The specific items for the Short Assessment Outline were extracted from the more intensive, comprehensive study. This reduction included sufficient information to get us the highlights of the social development of each child, so that the children could be placed in the appropriate developmental groupings. We found that by using the Short Assessment Outline, we could obtain a valid and reliable evaluation of the child's social developmental status, comparable to that obtained from the more extensive clinical study.[1]

1. See Appendix B for discussion of validity and reliability.

Criteria for Assessing
SOCIAL DEVELOPMENT

Relationship with Mother

Phase	Characteristic, expected, typical	Uncharacteristic, unexpected, atypical, pathological	
		Ranging from:	To:
Infant: birth to 1½ (Oral Phase)	First half-year, need-fulfilling relationship. Mother exists only for child's satisfaction; may be seen only as instrument to provide for satisfaction of needs. Child "wants" to be given everything and depends on mother for gratification.	Predominantly clinging relationship; seeking to get needs satisfied. Wants to be given to without making efforts.	Has given up trying to get needs satisfied. Has turned away from mother; apathetic; aloof. May rebuff her, refuse her help.
	One-half to one-and-one half years, may see mother as powerful object to influence in order to get what is needed; may make efforts to please or win her. Fears loss of mother. Establishes trust.	Constantly needs mother's presence, support, assurance; continually seeks contact. Appears overdependent, passive, obedient, overcompliant. Often insecure, apprehensive, tense, anxious in relating to mother.	May appear precociously independent or may have turned to another adult as mother-substitute. Difficult for mother to satisfy. Demanding, insistent, complaining, impatient in relation to mother. Greedy, insatiable; acts as if there is feeling of deprivation. Lack of trust.
Toddler: 1½ to 3 (Anal Phase)	Relationship with negativistic tinge. Control an important factor. At times may torment, harass, tease. Much ambivalence, sometimes love predominating, sometimes hate. Fears loss of mother's love. Negativism with insistence that mother be around. Object is needed to be there though child says "No."	Extremely controlling with mother. Dominating and bossy.	Extremely negativistic and defiant, with much strain in the relationship. "Difficult." Interaction intense, urgent, with much ambivalence. Quarrelsome, stubborn, obstinate. May torment or harass, with angry interaction and conflict. Frequent arguing, fault-finding, scolding, interrupting, provoking, teasing
		Extremely sensitive to mother's criticism. Cries easily. Feelings easily hurt by mother.	

Phase	Characteristic, expected, typical	Uncharacteristic, unexpected, atypical, pathological	
		Ranging from:	To:
Differentiating Stage: 3 to 4½ (Phallic Phase)	Developing awareness of his/her own sex identity; may affect some interaction with mother. Bids for mother's attention, admiration, and praise. Tries to show mother how big, attractive, powerful he/she is. Responsive to mother; more or less cooperative. Relationship mutually satisfying.	Overly concerned about sex identity; uses it in exaggerated attempts to get mother's attention, admiration, and praise. Constantly showing mother how big, attractive and powerful he/she is — to get reassurance, approval. Overly responsive, cooperative.	Indifferent to sex identity; denies any interest in mother; actively avoids her. Avoids attention and/or praise from mother; may even reject mother's attentions. Emphasizes smallness, powerlessness. Unresponsive, uncooperative.
Family Integration: Boy 4½ to 6 (Oedipal Phase).	With increasing awareness of his own sex identity, more seductive with mother and more possessive of her. May identify with father and act protective with mother. Copies father's behavior toward mother. May show some concern about whether mother prefers father or him. Shows preference for mother rather than father. May play parents against each other. Objects to parents going out together. Friend-	Extremely possessive with mother — rivalrous with father or siblings for mother; jealous of contacts mother has with others. Extremely seductive with mother, almost in caricatured, exaggerated ways. Has to show mother he is better than father and that father is no good. Adores and idealizes mother. Exaggerates masculine behavior, in relating to mother. Excessive interest in and sensitivity to mother's	Inhibits all contact with mother. Fearful of winning mother in competition with father. Fearful of retaliation by father if wins mother; avoids mother because of the danger. Great concern to show he is *not* a man, cannot win mother, is different from father. Inhibits masculine behavior in relating to mother. Lack of interest in or sensitivity to mother's feelings, moods. Lack of concern for mother's well-being.
			Masochistic — provoking retaliation, hurting by mother; sadistic — cruel. May be destructive (I hate you and don't love you).

Phase	Characteristic, expected, typical	Uncharacteristic, unexpected, atypical, pathological	
		Ranging from:	To:
	ly to mother; easily accepts her authority; turns to her when necessary for help. Shows some interest in and sensitivity to mother's feelings, moods. Shows some concern for mother's well-being.	feelings, moods. Extreme concern for mother's well-being.	
Family Integration: Girl 4½ to 6 (Oedipal Phase)	With increasing awareness of her own sex identity, more competitive with mother for father. May show some hostility toward mother; but also fear of retaliation and fear of hurting mother (who is also a love object). May anticipate being harmed by mother. Tries to be like mother, identify with her but to show her up; or may inhibit feminine behavior and appear tomboyish. May show some anxiety about being separated from mother because of own wishful fantasies. Objects to parents going out together. May play parents against each other. Shows some interest in and sensitivity to mother's feelings, moods. Shows some concern for mother's well-being.	Great concern that father prefers her to mother, that she is "better" than mother. Exaggerates own femininity. Extremely rivalrous with mother. Lacks concern about mother's well-being. Lacks interest in or sensitivity to mother's feelings, moods. Avoids mother.	Fearful about competing with mother; fearful of retaliation by mother, so actively avoids contact with father. Shows perference for mother rather than father. Great concern to show she is not a woman, cannot win father, is different from mother. Inhibits all feminine behavior. Intense anxiety about separation because of own fantasies. Excessive interest in and sensitivity to mother's feelings, moods. Extreme concern for mother's well-being.

Separation–Individuation

Phase	Characteristic, expected, typical	Uncharacteristic, unexpected, atypical, pathological	
		Ranging from:	To:
Infant: birth to 1½ (Oral Phase)	First half year, no clear differentiation of self. Sense of identity undeveloped and fluid — as if mother (or mother-substitute) should know his wishes-needs and meet them. Mother exists only for child's satisfaction of needs. No existence of her own. Depends on mother for gratification; Mother's other concerns or activities are experienced as rejection-desertion.	Establishment of identity continues undeveloped and fluid; no clear differentiation of self even begins. Needs to be given everything and does not make efforts to satisfy own needs. Great dependency. Little interest in "the world"; little or no attempt to reach out for anything; seldom manipulates things; "shuts out" the world.	Cannot tolerate separation. Exclusive in relating to mother; able to have relationship *only* with mother. Great anxiety when mother is not present.
	One-half to one-and-one-half, beginning to notice "the world" — reach out for and handle what is seen; respond to surroundings — sounds, sights. Beginning to distinguish between self and world around him. Can accept brief separation from mother, after some protest. Some object constancy, so positive image of mother maintained. Differentiates known from unknown. Beginning to develop ability to accept mother-substitutes (either other family members or familiar baby-sitters).		*Or,* has turned away from mother. Feels he cannot get needs satisfied by her or get what he wants. May appear unresponsive to her. May avoid contact with mother, rebuff her. No difficulty separating from mother. Has abandoned her, rejected her ("I don't want you because you don't satisfy my needs, don't give me love.").

Phase	Characteristic, expected, typical	Uncharacteristic, unexpected, atypical, pathological	
		Ranging from:	To:
Toddler: 1½ to 3 (Anal Phase)	Aware of self as separate from others — trying to control others and/or trying not to be controlled by others. Aware of some of own wants, likes and dislikes. May talk about self as a third person ("Betty wants that.") Looks at and describes self from viewpoint of (significant) others — e.g., "good boy." Able to leave mother and play by self in another room; can tolerate some distance from mother. Temporary separations from mother can be lengthened. Can move out toward other family members and familiar adults. Temporary separations from mother and home are possible, to go with familiar adult, such as grandparent.	Extreme concern about maintaining separateness — not being controlled by others. Avoids mother and/or other family members. Physically distant as much of the time as possible. Prefers to visit grandparents, neighbors; be with strangers.	Fear of being separate — tries to be "one" with more powerful being — desperately clings. Loses self in desire to be "good," not lose love and acceptance of mother and/or other family members. More aware of approval-disapproval of mother and family than of own wants-likes.
Differentiating Stage: 3 to 4½ (Phallic Phase)	Aware of own sexual identity. Enjoys mother's presence but can accept being separated from rest of family and from home. After short transition period, can accept attending nursery school. Can exchange visits at homes of peers.	Individuation only in terms of sex; exaggeration of sexual identification; confusion re sexual identification; denial of sexual identification. Uses separation from mother-family-home to deny fears, weaknesses, vulnerability; prove strength, power, "bigness," courage. Too easily	Uses inability to separate from mother-family-home to deny "growing up," power, strength; emphasizes smallness, helplessness. Unable to accept nursery school — unless mother stays with him all the time. Unable to visit peers.

Phase	Characteristic, expected, typical	Uncharacteristic, unexpected, atypical, pathological	
		Ranging from:	To:
Family Integration: 4½ to 6 (Oedipal Phase)	Aware of identification with and competition with same-sex parent; aware of identification with family — as a member of the family. Able to attend school regularly; able to accept overnight visits to homes of friends. Becoming aware of self as a member of the community. Identification with peers at school. Able to attend day-camp; be away from home for a weekend.	Overidentifies with same-sex parent; overidentifies with family. Not aware of other facets of individuation. Avoids mother or father because of danger from rivalry. Avoids family — away from home most of the time.	Intense anxiety about separation because of own fantasies. Has to stay near mother-family-home because of what might happen while he is gone. Unable to attend school regularly; unable to stay away from home overnight.

Criteria for Assessing
SOCIAL DEVELOPMENT

Relationship with Father

Phase	Characteristic, expected, typical	Uncharacteristic, unexpected, atypical, pathological	
		Ranging from:	To:
Infant: birth to 1½ (Oral Phase)	Recognition of father; some contact with father, and responsive to overtures from father, though may prefer mother as caretaking person.	No relationship with father; unaware of father; unresponsive to father; uninvolved with him at all. Rejects father, pushes him away.	Clings to father, continually seeking contact with father. Relates to father as mother-substitute, to depend on and get his needs satisfied, give him affection. Prefers father to mother as caretaking person. Submissive, dependent, overcompliant with father. Continually tries to please father, get his approval and/or sympathy. Demanding of father; difficult to satisfy.
Toddler: 1½ to 3 (Anal Phase)	Relationship with father predominately friendly. Enjoys being with father, but can accept being separated from him. Some struggle re control; may try to boss, tell father what to do and how; may argue, defy.	Minimal contact with father. Fearful of father, apprehensive, cautious, timid; shy. Anticipates father will not like him or accept him, and avoids father. Relationship with father appears transitory, shallow, superficial.	Unfriendly, extremely negativistic. Relationship intense, urgent, with much strain and anxiety. Child characteristically has angry interaction or conflict with father. Frequent arguing, finding fault, scolding, provoking, teasing. Extremely defiant, difficult, quarrelsome, hostile, stubborn, obstinate in relating to father. Masochistic — provoking retaliation, getting hurt by father; sadistic — cruel.

Phase	Characteristic, expected, typical	Uncharacteristic, unexpected, atypical, pathological	
		Ranging from:	To:
Differentiating Stage: 3 to 4½ (Phallic Phase)	Developing awareness of his/her own sexual identity may affect interaction with father. Continued bids for father's attention, admiration, and praise. Tries to show father how big, attractive, powerful he/she is. Boy may anticipate being harmed (castrated) by father. Responsive to father; more or less cooperative with father. Relationship mutually satisfying.	Uses sexual identity in exaggerated attempts to get father's attention, admiration, and praise. Constantly showing father how big, attractive and powerful he/she is — to get reassurance, approval. Overly responsive to father; overly cooperative.	Indifferent to sexual identity; denies any interest in father; actively avoids him. Avoids attention and/or praise from father may even reject father's attentions. Emphasizes smallness, powerlessness. Unresponsive, uncooperative with father.
Family Integration: Boy 4½ to 6 (Oedipal Phase)	With increasing awareness of his own sexual identity, more competitive with father for mother. May show some hostility toward father, but also fear of retaliation and fear of hurting father (who is also a love object). Tries to be like father, identify with him but to show him up; or may inhibit masculine behavior. May show some anxiety about being separated from father because of own wishful fantasies. Objects to parents going out together. May play parents against each other. Shows some interest in and sensitivity to father's feelings.	Great concern to show mother prefers him to father, that he is "better" than father. "Puts down" father. Exaggerates own masculinity. Extremely rivalrous with father. Shows much hostility to father. Lacks any concern about father's well-being. Lacks any interest in or sensitivity to father's feelings. Avoids father.	Fearful of competing with father; fearful of retaliation by father; so actively avoids contact with mother. Shows preference for father rather than mother. Great concern to show he is not a man, cannot win mother, is different from father. Inhibits all masculine behavior. Intense anxiety about separation because of own fantasies. Excessive interest in and sensitivity to father's feelings, moods. Extreme concern for father's well-being.

Phase	Characteristic, expected, typical	Uncharacteristic, unexpected, atypical, pathological	
		Ranging from:	To:
	moods. Shows some concern for father's well-being. Shows preference for mother rather than father.		
Family Integration: Girl 4½ to 6 (Oedipal Phase)	With increasing awareness of her won sexual identity, more seductive with father and more possessive of him. May identify with mother and act solicitous with father. Copies mother's behavior toward father. May show some concern about whether father prefers mother or her. Shows preference for father rather than mother. May play parents against each other. Objects to parents going out together. Friendly to father; easily accepts his authority; turns to him when necessary for help. Shows some interest in and sensitivity to father's feelings, moods. Shows some concern for father's well-being.	Extremely possessive with father — rivalrous with mother or siblings for father; jealous of contacts father has with others. Extremely seductive with father, almost in caricatured, exaggerated ways. *Has* to show father she is better than mother and that mother is no good. Adores and idealizes father. Exaggerates feminine behavior in relating to father. Excessive interest in and sensitivity to father's feelings, moods. Extreme concern for father's well-being.	Consciously inhibits all contact with father. Fearful of winning father in competition with mother. Fearful of retaliation by mother if wins father; avoids father because of the danger. Great concern to show she is *not* a woman, cannot win father, is different from mother. Inhibits feminine behavior in relation to father. Lack of interest in or sensitivity to father's feelings, moods. Lack of concern for father's well-being.

SOCIAL DEVELOPMENT

Relationship with Siblings

Phase	Characteristic, expected, typical	Uncharacteristic, unexpected, atypical, pathological	
		Ranging from:	To:
Infant: birth to 1½ (Oral Phase)	Recognition of siblings; some contact with them, responsive to overtures from siblings; some interest in their activities. At times tries to imitate, copy, sibling behaviors.	No relationship with siblings; unaware of them; unresponsive to them; uninvolved with them in any way; no interest in their activities. Rejects siblings, pushes them away.	Relates to siblings as mother-substitute, to depend on and get needs satisfied; prefers sibling to mother as caretaking person. Always plays "baby" with sibling. Submissive, dependent, overcompliant. Continually tries to please siblings, get their approval and/or sympathy. Clinging with siblings. Demanding of siblings; difficult to satisfy.
Toddler: 1½ to 3 (Anal Phase)	Enjoys being with siblings, but can accept being separated from them. Some struggle re control; may try to boss them, tell them what to do and how; may try to control by "mothering." May argue, provoke, tease at times.	Fearful of siblings, apprehensive, cautious, timid, shy. Avoids contact with siblings. Anticipates siblings will not like him and/or accept him. Relationship with siblings appears transitory, shallow, superficial.	Usually in conflict with siblings. Unfriendly, extremely negativistic. Relationship intense, urgent, with much strain and anxiety. Angry interaction, frequent arguing, finding fault, scolding, provoking, teasing. Extremely defiant, difficult, quarrelsome, hostile, stubborn, obstinate.

Phase	Characteristic, expected, typical	Uncharacteristic, unexpected, atypical, pathological	
		Ranging from:	To
Differentiating Stage: 3 to 4½ (Phallic Phase)	Can participate in some play with siblings, can take turns and share. Asserts self with siblings, but shows some sensitivity to needs and feelings of siblings. Competes with siblings for attention and for toys. Feels "close" to same-sex sibling. May engage in sex play with sibling.	Inhibits self-assertion with siblings. Overly concerned about taking turns, sharing. Inhibits competition with siblings; "Too nice" with siblings; "too generous." Extremely sensitive to needs and feelings of siblings.	Extremely competitive with siblings, in all areas. Extremely assertive with siblings. No sensitivity to needs and feelings of siblings.
Family Integration: 4½ to 6 (Oedipal Phase)	Reciprocal relations with siblings. "Family" play with siblings. Can lead or follow. Easily shares, takes turns. Friendly, responsive, cooperative with siblings, most of the time. Shows interest in and sensitivity to siblings' moods. Shows concern for siblings' well-being.	Excessive interest in and sensitivity to siblings' feelings, moods. Extreme concern for siblings' well-being.	Relates as if much younger child, using techniques of earlier phases. No interest in or sensitivity to siblings' feelings, moods. No concern for siblings' well-being.

SOCIAL DEVELOPMENT

Relationship with Teacher

Phase	Characteristic, expected, typical	Uncharacteristic, unexpected, atypical, pathological	
		Ranging from:	To:
Infant: birth to 1½ (Oral Phase)	Relates to teacher as a mother-substitute, to depend on and get his needs satisfied, to give him care and affection.	Completely unresponsive to teacher; uninvolved with teacher. Apathetic, withdrawn. Distant in relating to teacher.	Overdependent on teacher; excessively clinging; constantly trying to get contact, sympathy, attention. Does not individualize teachers. Overly demanding, insistent, impatient in relating to teacher. Difficult to satisfy; usually wants more than teacher can give; complaining.
Toddler: 1½ to 3 (Anal Phase)	Struggle for control with teacher. Tries to tell her what to do and how to do it. At times, bossy; at times may argue, defy, be negativistic.	Fearful of teacher, apprehensive, cautious, timid, shy. Anticipates teacher will not like him or accept him and actively avoids teacher. Relationship may appear transitory, shallow, superficial.	Unfriendly to teacher; extremely negativistic, defiant. Quarrelsome with teacher; hostile, stubborn, obstinate. "Difficult" child. Much angry interaction and conflict with teacher; arguing, finding fault, scolding, provoking, teasing.
Differentiating Stage: 3 to 4½ (Phallic Phase)	At times may try to identify with teacher and be like her; at other times may compete with teacher. Bids for teacher's attention, admiration, praise. Able to assert own desires and ideas to teacher. Able to ask for help.	Extremely competitive with teacher. Overidentifies with teacher. Constantly seeking teacher's attention — e.g., by clowning, "acting up," "being difficult," "showing off," making excessive demands. Extremely assertive with teacher.	Ignores teacher. Avoids teacher's attention. Unable to assert himself with teacher, unable to make desires and needs known.

Phase	Characteristic, expected, typical	Uncharacteristic, unexpected, atypical, pathological	
		Ranging from:	To:
Family Integration: 4½ to 6 (Oedipal Phase)	Friendly in relating to teacher. Usually responsive, cooperative. Easily accepts teacher's authority and teacher's help. With awareness of his own sexual identity, boy may act "gallant," "charming," "seductive" with teacher. Girl may be coy. Shows some interest in and sensitivity to teacher's feelings, moods. Shows some concern for teacher's well-being.	Overly friendly with teacher; overly cooperative; "too nice." Has to accept teacher's authority and teacher's help. Excessive interest in and sensitivity to teacher's feelings, moods. Extreme concern for teacher's well-being.	Avoids teacher; makes active effort to stay at a distance from teacher. Unresponsive to teacher. Will not accept teacher's authority or teacher's help. No interest in or sensitivity to teacher's feelings, moods. No concern for teacher's well-being.

Relationship with Other Children

Phase	Characteristic, expected, typical	Uncharacteristic, unexpected, atypical, pathological	
		Ranging from:	To:
Infant: birth to 1½ (Oral Phase)	Notices other children. Some interest in other children for brief periods of time — as an observer. Some response to overtures of other children. Characteristically, spends most of the time playing with own hands and feet, materials, toys and/or equipment, household items. Other children show some interest in him; give some attention to him; make some overtures toward him.	Completely unresponsive to other children, uninterested in them, uninvolved with them. Unrelated to other children. Apathetic, withdrawn. Rejects other children ; pushes them away. Most of the time in solitary play, physically and emotionally distant from other children — "isolated." May wander around alone, aimless, with no focus. Most of the time this child has no effect on other children. They are oblivious to him or not interested in him; They ignore him.	Relates to other children as mother-substitute to depend on and get needs satisfied. Always a "baby," always a "follower." Submissive, dependent, overcompliant, clinging, with other children. Continually tries to please, get their approval and/or sympathy. Demands more than other children are willing to give. Other children try to avoid him. Sees other children as treating him unfairly, picking on him. Complaining.
Toddler: 1½ to 3 (Anal Phase)	Some struggle with other children for control; tries to tell them what to do and how to do it. May try to take the "authority" role, or to control by "mothering." At times bossy, at times arguing. Most of the time in play parallel to other children. May play alone, but next to another child and may be doing same things as other child. Much of the time this child arouses interest of other children who may watch his activity.	Fearful, apprehensive, cautious, timid in relating to other children. Feels other children will not like him or accept him; avoids them. Shy. Lack of interaction; distant with other children. Avoids all fights or arguments. Any relationships with other children appear transitory, shallow, superficial. Very controlled, inhibited in play with other children. Cannot "let himself go."	Unfriendly in relating to other children. Defiant, negativistic, quarrelsome, hostile. Frequent angry interaction and conflict; frequent arguing, finding fault, scolding, interrupting, provoking, teasing. Bullies other children; makes them cry. Sadistic, cruel. Torturing possessiveness. Masochistic — provokes other children to hurt him. Easily offended by other children.

Phase	Characteristic, expected, typical	Uncharacteristic, unexpected, atypical, pathological	
		Ranging from:	To:
Differentiating Stage: 3 to 4½ (Phallic Phase)	Can participate in play with other children. Asserts self, but also shows some sensitivity to needs and feelings of other children. Competes with other children for attention and for toys. Spends most of his time with one child who is special friend, but may also spend time with other children, or some time alone. Shows some social skills. Exchanges visits with other children. Much of the time, he arouses interest of other children who may try to participate with him in ongoing activity. Some children seek him out as playmate.	Inhibits self-assertion with other children. Inhibits competitiveness with other children. Extremely sensitive to needs and feelings of other children. "Too generous," "too nice."	Extremely assertive with other children. Extremely competitive with other children. No sensitivity to needs and feelings of other children. Much of the time stimulates other children by his activity to point where they may act in an excited, uncontrolled way. Often has disruptive effect.
Family Integration: 4½ to 6 (Oedipal Phase)	Reciprocal relations with other children. Constancy and depth in relationships. Friendly, responsive, cooperative. Increasing social sensitivity, increasing social skills, sympathetic. Can lead or follow. Most of the time a participant in cooperative play with another child or a small group of children. Boys may prefer to play with other boys and girls with other girls. However, much more "family play" with girls	Avoiding play with same-sex children; preferring to play with opposite sex children. *Has* to be leader.	Relates as if much younger child, using techniques of earlier phases. Can *only* be a follower.

SOCIAL DEVELOPMENT

Participation in Groups of Children

Phase	Characteristic, expected, typical	Uncharacteristic, unexpected, atypical, pathological	
		Ranging from:	To:
Infant: birth to 1½ (Oral Phase)	May passively participate just by being present in the same situation with other children.		
Toddler: 1½ to 3 (Anal Phase)	Sometimes interested in ongoing activities of a small group; occasionally can function in a group situation.	*Has* to get into the group. Pushes himself into groups. Becomes overexcited and overstimulated by group and may act in uncontrolled way. Erratic group participation.	Avoids groups and/or not interested in groups. Minimal participation in groups. Cannot function as a member of a group and/or does not become involved in group activities. May be oblivious to group; or fearful and anxious.
Differentiating Stage: 3 to 4½ (Phallic Phase)	Much of the time can function adequately as a member of a group. Can participate actively, making contributions, offering ideas or suggestions. Alert and responsive in discussions. Active in some group projects.	Cannot function well in group — too assertive, too competitive; alienates other children in group. Unable to function cooperatively. Tries unsuccessfully to manipulate other group participants.	Passive observer in group. Unable to take initiative; unable to arouse the interest of other members of group.
Family Integration: 4½ to 6 (Oedipal Phase)	Most of the time he is in small group situations with two or three other children. Participates actively as group member, cooperates with others. Creative in group situation; invents new play. Can lead at times, follow at times.	*Has* to be a leader in the group. Tries to be "autocratic parent." Does not know how to charm others in group into accepting his ideas.	Sterotyped, unoriginal in group play. Copies other group members; cannot originate group activities. Can function in group as a follower. Denies interest in group and/or avoids group.

Chapter 4
Emotional Development

The child usually begins life with a cry, which is his response to the changing environment from intrauterine life to birth. From the beginning of life onward, however, he not only reacts emotionally to his environment, but he also expresses various emotions which influence his relationships with others. During the early months of life, the feeling-tones are limited in number; they move from comfort to discomfort, from pain to contentment. However, as with other areas of development, differentiation gradually occurs in the emotional area.

The mood of the child, the affective tone in which the child explores the outside world and responds to it—for example, while sucking or bathing—is a most important guide to the child's general development. In fact, any one of the child's expressions of emotion is an indicator to the environment about the child's well-being or feelings of discomfort.

Every action of the child occurs within the context of a feeling-tone, and often the feeling-tone is important because it will organize subsequent behavior and influence the child's thinking and interactions with others. The feeling-tones during the early years often are confirmed by the mother as she expresses her own feelings of happiness or of concern, and this interplay slowly brings about an orchestration of feelings.

The expressions of feelings and the way others respond to these expressions may indicate whether the child is developing appropriately; and it is most interesting in this regard to have learned from our study that the parents and teachers, as well as the research staff, gave the child's emotional tone—that is, whether a child is happy or sad, anxious or angry—a most significant role in assessing the children throughout the several years of the study.

Characteristic Mood

We discovered that it was important to assess the characteristic mood of a child because of the impact this mood may have on other aspects of development. By *characteristic mood* we mean that mood which is specific for a given child and which is most typical over a period of time for the child. It is one of his outstanding characteristics. The child's mood gives a quality to his individuality typical for him. It is significant whether he is characteristically happy-contented-satisfied or characteristically depressed-unhappy-disappointed; characteristically anxious-fearful-apprehensive or characteristically angry-annoyed-irritated. For instance, any child may show transient episodes of anxiety or fear, but if anxiety is the child's characteristic affect, this will influence his interactions with others and his subsequent development in all areas. Therefore, in assessing a child, it is relevant to note whether he conveys a feeling of hope and confidence; or of despair, hopelessness and discouragement; or of constant anxiety.

In general, adults are aware of the characteristic emotional tone of a child and can verbalize their awareness in response to questioning. In fact, observers may often be able to detect the relationships of these characteristic moods to specific situations, such as sleeping or toilet training or special social interaction.

Variety and Range of Emotions

With maturation, it is expected that children will develop and show an increasing differentiation in the variety and range of emotions experienced and expressed. But although we have many techniques for measuring the increasing intellectual capacity of the child, we have been less successful in developing techniques for measuring the increasing differentiating capacity as to affects.

At first, the infant experiences pleasure and pain. Periods of tension-irritability are followed by periods of contentment when his needs are satisfied. Somewhat later during infancy, he may give a smile of recognition and happiness when he sees persons he "knows." By his sounds and movements, he gives signs of enjoyment as he exercises his voice, manipulates objects, and experiments with gestures. He laughs easily in response to others' noddings or other motions and in response to another's laughter. He laughs during various physical activities or when he is played with or during social contacts with others. He begins to show some feelings of trust as well as some affection.

There may also be indications of feelings of bewilderment or puzzlement or frustration, obvious signs when something "hurts" him, and at times indications that he is experiencing anxiety. Very young children may have an anxiety response to strangers, which is attributable to a fear of the unknown, or anxiety about the loss of someone who was present. Similarly, the child may show a happy response to the reappearance of someone who had seemed to disappear. Thus, in the peek-a-boo game (or the hide-and-seek game which children play later) there is both the anxiety of loss and the happiness of reunification.

During the toddler phase of development, there are more lively feelings—enthusiasm, interest, and joy. Much of the time, there are strong, "peak" feelings. The toddler will show pleasure in movement, exploration, and "functions lust." Sudden outbursts of anger may occur but are over quickly. There are some expressions of guilt and shame and perhaps the beginnings of some social feelings.

Later, a whole range of complex feelings come into being. By nursery-school age, emotional behavior has been differentiated to the extent that one can observe expressions of hope, disappointment, joy, envy, pride, self-consciousness, friendliness, and unfriendliness.

Fears may be expressed in the early years of life. At first, fears of noises, strange persons, and strange situations. These gradually decrease, and fears of imaginary, anticipated, and supernatural dangers subsequently appear. Also, there are fears of being physically harmed and occasionally the fear of death. We know that throughout the differentiating (phallic) and family integration (oedipal) phases, the most common fears are of doctors, dogs, storms, and darkness, though ghosts and witches may also be feared at times. And we find that at night the fears are intensified.

During the early years, we may see signs of anxiety centered around parent-child relationships and later around peer relationships. As the child becomes older we observe also an increase in anger overtly directed toward a particular source. In nursery school and kindergarten, the major cause of anger appears to be conflict with other children, especially conflicts over play-things. However, children also become angry when there is interference with their activities and when there are problems with self-help; and occasionally there may be anger because of conflict with the authority figures in the schoolroom.

In addition to the variety of feeling-tones, we can also observe individual characteristics for each child in the range of feelings. Some children stay in the middle of a comparatively comfortable feeling-tone, where neither the anger nor the happiness reaches great intensity. They are comparatively calm in affect, and in discharge pattern stay in the middle range. Other children tend toward intense discharge patterns, and, therefore, their anger or their happiness seems to be of greater significance. They show their feelings very clearly and communicate with the outside world with intensity in a wide range of emotions.

Emotional Expression

In the earliest months, children express their feelings directly through body movements, laughter, crying, and facial expressions, such as smiling or grimacing, and through the sounds they make. Affect is likely to be quite labile, with sudden changes and frequent tantrums.

There is then a development from the immediate expression of feelings—from sudden outbursts to delayed expression. Feelings begin to come "under control." There is a decrease in the random discharge of emotion and an increase in the purposive "directing" of expression. Children exhibit an increasing mastery of the "chaotic state within," along with increasing mastery of the affect expressed. They gradually move from uncontrolled, immediate, motor (global) expression of affect to more controlled, delayed, verbal expression.

As they mature, children show an increase in the stability of their emotions, as well as a decrease in the intensity of expression. During the nursery-school and kindergarten years, it is expected that emotional life will become more or less stable, though occasional outbursts and displays of anger will still occur.

The more diffuse, uninhibited expressions, such as screaming or agitated movements, are replaced by verbal techniques, such as describing, questioning, and explaining. Anxiety responses, which earlier were expresed in random movement and discharge patterns, may become channeled. Crying as a response to situations that are frustrating and/or overwhelming, decreases between infancy and the kindergarten years, though it occasionally is still somewhat in evidence. Some children may continue to have temper problems, such as stamping of the feet, hitting, and throwing oneself to the floor. But these more diffuse, uninhibited expressions of anger tend to be replaced by such verbal techniques as name-calling, threatening, teasing, and belittling.

It is of interest that sex differences appear early. At all ages, our research study found boys showing more angry outbursts than girls and expressing anger more aggressively than girls.

As children become increasingly aware of and verbal about their feelings, they are able to recognize more and more different feelings and to give them their appropriate names. Instead of just saying, "I feel good" or "I don't feel good," they can differentiate "good" in terms of "I feel glad," or "That makes me happy," or "I'm so excited" and "not good" in terms of "I don't like that," or "I feel mad," or "That makes me sad."

Although there is a certain amount of expressive freedom, the child is learning to meet cultural expectations of *what* is appropriate and what is inappropriate to express, *when and where* it is appropriate to express which feelings, and *how* it is appropriate to express specific feelings. Simultaneously, there is an increase in the conscious use of culturally approved gestures, postures, facial expressions, and statements about feelings.

Social Orientation

Just as in the child's social development there was increasing concern for others and increasing capacity to share with them, in the emotional development of the child there is also an increasingly social orientation.

The maturing child moves from being completely self-centered (insensitive to the feelings of others and their responses to his actions and his expressions of feelings) to becoming more sensitive to others' moods, hurts, joys, irritations, and feelings about him. As he becomes older, the child gradually shows more sympathy, compassion, pity, and tenderness to others. At the same time, he also becomes more aware of others' responses to him, and consequently he may anticipate responses that contribute to his own feelings of shame, guilt, and embarrassment.

Assessment of Emotional Development

As noted earlier, emotional development was considered significant by adults and often was mentioned spontaneously by parents and teachers in interviews about the children. This, then, is another area that can be assessed in a more systematic way by those who do not have clinical training. It does not require a shift in the adults' accustomed ways of observing children and describing them.

Rather than requiring clinicians or nonclinicians to count specific behaviors, our emphasis in this aspect of development, as with social development, is to elicit a broad, overall judgment as to developmental progression.

The items that were included in the final Short Assessment Outline were selected from the more comprehensive outline used in the intensive clinical study. The various statistical analyses had shown that, taken together, these particular items offered a valid and reliable indication of the child's emotional developmental status.[1]

---

1. See Appendix B for discussion of validity and reliability.

Criteria for Assessing
EMOTIONAL DEVELOPMENT

Variety and Intensity of Affect; Characteristic Mood

Phase	Characteristic, expected, typical	Uncharacteristic, unexpected, atypical, pathological	
		Ranging from:	To:
Infant: birth to 1½ (Oral Stage)	Periods of tension (pain)-irritability followed by periods of contentment (pleasure). Glow of contentment when satiated and needs met. Most of the time conveys sense of general comfort. Occasional indications of frustration-anger; anxiety. Beginning to show some feelings of trust, some affection.	Persistent, unrelieved tension (pain) — irritability, with subsequent anger (rage) and/or exhaustion. Most of the time irritable, cranky, fussy, restless, discontented, uncomfortable. Frequent signs of frustration-anger.	Chronically depressed, dejected, or apathetic. Most of the time unresponsive, listless, air of hopelessness. Indifferent.
Toddler: 1½ to 3 (Anal Phase)	Child is able to experience and to express some variety of feelings. Much of the time, strong "peak" feelings; excited, lively kinds of feelings — enthusiasm, interest, joy. Unpleasant moods or sudden outbursts may occasionally occur, but are soon over.	Extreme intensities of feelings are experienced; high levels of tension. Shifts from extremes of "high" and "low." Great excitability. Rages. Much disgust. Strong reactions to control by others. Outbursts frequently occur and may last a long while, in attempts to control others. Characteristic mood is angry, attacking, annoyed, resentful.	Child is able to experience and to express only a limited variety of feelings. Child expresses primarily one or two feelings. Some feelings are *seldom* experienced or expressed; some feelings are "never" experienced or expressed (i.e., certain affect is repressed, inhibited, denied). Child may appear bland, sullen, solemn.

Phase	Characteristic, expected, typical	Uncharacteristic, unexpected, atypical, pathological	
		Ranging from:	To:
Differentiating Stage: 3 to 4½ (Phallic Phase)	Increasing differentiation in the variety of feelings experienced and expressed. Child is able to experience a moderate range of affect — more so with his own family than with other people. Somewhat subdued feelings; experience of affect is mild. Characteristic mood is satisfied, content, pleased, happy. Evidence of some feelings of embarrassment, shame, self-consciousness.	Extremely strong, intense emotions. Rage, fury. Characteristic mood is attacking, "hyper"-active.	Child is able to experience a small range of affect; little variety of affect. Child has little awareness of variation in feelings. Characteristic mood is anxious, apprehensive, fearful, insecure and/or joyless, unhappy, sad, disappointed. Affect is inhibited or restricted, so that child is unaware of variation in feelings.
Family Integration: 4½ to 6 (Oedipal Phase)	Great differentiation in the variety of feelings experienced and expressed. Expressions of tenderness, pity, sympathy, compassion beginning to appear; also guilt. Sensitive to others' feelings and responses.	Extreme feelings.	Extreme constriction of feelings. Lack of feelings for others.

Criteria for Assessing
EMOTIONAL DEVELOPMENT

Expression of Affect

Phase	Characteristic, expected, typical	Uncharacteristic, unexpected, atypical, pathological	
		Ranging from:	To:
Infant: Birth to 1½ (Oral Phase)	Affect expressed immediately. Undifferentiated, global responses. Expression of feelings often with whole body. Also, smiling, crying, grimacing; making of sounds, agitated movements.	Cries easily. Violent display of undirected energy. Screaming, kicking, holding breath, hitting head against wall or furniture, biting self.	Subdued expression of affect. Whimpering, moaning, whining, silent staring.
Toddler: 1½ to 3 (Anal Phase)	At times, short delay in expression. Expression of feelings is in actions more than in words — in body movements, gestures, smiling, crying. Occasionally child may say he feels "good" or "not good." Child is able to express some variations in feelings.	Uncontrolled in expressing affect. Unable to delay expression — affect is expressed immediately and with great intensity, e.g., screaming, throwing self on floor, agitated movement (temper tantrums), throwing things. Explosions of messy, destructive behavior; fury.	Feelings are expressed by brooding, sulking, whining. Outbursts rarely occur. Unpleasant moods may persist for long periods. Child primarily expresses one or two feelings.
Differentiating Stage: 3 to 4½ (Phallic Phase)	Some verbal expression of feelings, e.g., I'm mad, I'm happy. Also, conscious use of gestures, postures, facial expressions, body movements, to express feelings. Feelings expressed openly and directly (girls less open than boys in expressing feelings). A "settling down" for both sexes in expression of feelings.	Feelings may be expressed in an artificial, exaggerated way. Child "overdramatizes" expression of feelings, is histrionic as a way of getting attention, of exhibiting self, showing off. Affect is labile; rapid and sudden shifts. Expression of affect may seem inappropriate to the precipitating conditions or to the ongoing	Child expresses some affect, but there is restraint, guardedness, hesitation — within the family, as well as outside. Affect is inhibited or restricted. Feelings may be expressed indirectly or in devious ways, e.g., in fantasy. Unhappy moods may persist for unusually long periods of time. (More often seen with girls than with boys at

Phase	Characteristic, expected, typical	Uncharacteristic, unexpected, atypical, pathological	
		Ranging from:	To:
	Increasing mastery of the chaotic emotional states within; expression of affect can be delayed to some extent, is under better control. Expression of affect seems appropriate to the situation. Affect stable, though occasional outbursts occur. Displays of anger of short duration.	situation — either as an overreaction or as a "wrong" reaction. Affective expression is extreme and/or intense.	this age). Face may appear impassive, frozen. Feelings "held in."
Family Integration: 4½ to 6 (Oedipal Phase)	Increasingly able to express feelings verbally rather than in actions. Increasingly able to express a range of feelings with peers and teachers, as well as with own family members. Increasingly able to delay expression. Boys more often open or intense in expressing feelings than girls; boys more often open than at earlier age. Girls cry more than boys.	Regression to earlier ways of expressing feelings, e.g., nonverbal.	Child expresses only a very limited variety of feelings.

Chapter 5
Ego Development

The term *ego* refers to the functions that deal with the child's capacity to perceive and assess external and internal realities and to integrate them. This includes evaluation and adaptation. *Ego equipment* refers to capacities that permit the child to perceive internal and external realities. Perception, motility, speech, and cognitive functioning are part of the equipment of the child.

The child's ego permits him to learn from his experiences and to achieve his goals. Ego functions permit coordination of the demands of the child's own inner drives with the demands and pressures of the external world. Reality testing, as one of the functions of the ego, allows fantasies and wishes to be tested against external realities. An additional faculty of the ego is that of integrating the various psychic components and capacities and synthesizing them.

Motor Development

The child's motor discharge is part of his functioning from infancy, and there is much individual variation among children in this discharge. Some are more quiet, some more active. Some discharge primarily through action, while others are observers—"intakers" of the outside world. In addition, there are wide fluctuations in the competency of the children's performances.

It is through motor functioning that the child interacts with the outside world, though perceptual modalities such as touch, smell, vision, and hearing are contributing factors. His motor capacity permits the child to move in the direction of his interests, to stimulate the outside world in the direction he desires, and to change the outside world to some extent.

The child moves from complete dependence on the outside world for his physical needs and bodily care toward the beginning of mastery—turning, sitting, crawling, walking, and reaching out for and manipulating objects. He first learns to handle rattles, teething rings, stuffed animals, and toys, and later plays with push-and-pull toys. At the same time, he gains some control of his own body—feeding himself, toileting, and trying to dress and undress himself.

As the child progresses in motor development from crawling to walking, his whole world changes. Walking gives him a different view of the world, a different relationship to other persons. It means "separating from" and "moving toward." Instead of being passively a receiver, he can, if he chooses, be actively engaged with the environment.

Thus, motor development, as an aspect of ego development, can be considered in terms of its influence on other experiences of the child. In nursery schools or at home, the space and the facilities provided for the child to exercise his motor skills not only deal with his muscles and his central nervous system: They also provide opportunities for independence and experimentation to explore and to master body functions, as well as opportunities to learn to relate to and cooperate with others.

If there is unevenness in the child's development—for example, if a child is slow in his motor development but precocious in cognitive development or social development—this could lead to a feeling of discontent or failure. The child may understand more than he can translate into motor skills. On the other hand, a child may have extraordinary motor skills and consequently move, walk, and run before other aspects of development are ready for it. For example, he may find himself away from his mother—separated—before he is emotionally able to deal with it. Thus, a form of separation problem could result from such unevenness in development.

During the preschool and kindergarten years, the child's physical activity increases and becomes broader and smoother. He develops more control of his physical movements—his gross coordination and his fine eye/hand coordination. He becomes more agile and more poised in motor achievement; and his fine motor activities show more dexterity and more precision. Most of his activities are self-initiated, and he needs little help from others.

He may show off his physical skills and achievement with stunts, tricks, or "special performances." By nursery-school age, children spend much time running, jumping, climbing, and riding tricycles, adding their own unique frills to each of these activities. They are, however, also interested in the fine manipulations of play materials and in learning to button their sweaters or jackets and to lace their shoes.

By the time children arrive in kindergarten, they are even more accomplished. Their gross motor activity is well developed: They can skip, walk a straight line, and descend stairs alternating feet. And their fine motor activities are more precise: They can stitch with a needle and thread and use small scissors for precise cutting. However, motor development often depends on the interest shown by the environment, whether this aspect of development is stimulated or whether other modalities of ego activities are preferred.

Communication

At first the infant communicates by body movements, by noises, and by crying. Eventually he begins to use simple words and then one-word sentences.

As the child progresses in his development, he acquires more words and learns to use these words to communicate more effectively. He moves from egocentric to sociocentric speech, from thinking out loud to himself and engaging in monologues to directing his language toward others and trying to influence them. He talks more, and his speech becomes more comprehensible, more articulate, and grammatically more complex. He can use his langauge to express his needs and desires, describe events in which he participated or which he observed, exchange bits of information with those around him, ask questions, and tell others what to do.

Gradually, the child learns to use language to plan activities with others and to coordinate group activities. There is an increase in the use of complex forms of sentences and in the accurate use of abstract words.

As in the area of motor development, the emergence of speech shows great individual variation. Some children are early speakers and thus have available to them forms of communication with the outside world which permit the opening of new channels of inter-relationship. Other children start speaking a year or more later than the average and thus are limited in their interactions with others. There are children who are quite able to understand what is said to them but who are not yet able to respond verbally. This can bring about discontent, restlessness, and impatience, and unless those in the child's environment are able to recognize what is happening and to act on this in some way, there may be additional difficulties for the child.

Also, there are children who are precocious in their cognitive development and who are able to learn words and to accumulate a vocabulary, the use of which goes beyond their emotional capacity. Because they give the impression of being more advanced than they actually are, they may stimulate the environment to interact with them on a higher intellectual level, although they are functioning on a lower emotional level.

The significance, thus, from the viewpoint of ego development, is not so much just the acquisition of language but the role language plays in the child's social and emotional relationships. Therefore, language development needs to be examined as to its ego-appropriateness, its relationship to other areas of ego functioning, and its effect on other aspects of development.

Mental Development

Under the heading of "mental development" we refer to the individual's mental equipment—his curiosity, intelligence, creativity, judgment, anticipation, and planning. As part of his developmental progression, the child expands his capacity to perceive the world, explore it, and act on it. Behavior is increasingly organized, and yet can be adaptable and spontaneous. The child gradually displays more creativity in the use of materials and equipment. At the same time, he shows improvement in making judgments and decisions.

As an infant he begins to notice the world around him and to explore it. He handles objects, crawls, and pokes into corners. He is responsive to his surroundings—the sights, sounds, and smells.

As a toddler he expands his capacity to perceive the world and explore it. He will walk into various rooms in the house, climb to great heights, and wander in the park or into stores along the sidewalk.

Gradually, the child moves from concrete to abstract thinking; from perception to conception to explanation to inference; from magical to realistic thinking.[1] He is in contact with reality, although there is some fantasy. He becomes better able to differentiate between fantasy and reality.

He learns simple concepts of distance and space, such as near-far, on-under, next to, in front of, and in back of. He shows increasing interest in direction. He slowly develops time concepts, such as now-later-before, and number concepts, such as larger-smaller and more-less. He is interested also in the places where things "belong." And by nursery-school age, he can name the street on which he lives.

During nursery school and kindergarten, the child shows progression in learning and may compete with peers in this area. His attention span is increasing, as is his interest in asking questions and seeking answers. He becomes more involved in intellectual functioning and learning. He is eager to learn and seems to get satisfaction and pleasure from his intellectual achievements.

The intelligence of the child is an important ego function. Its assessment permits the adults in the child's environment to infer how much cognitive stimulation the child might respond to. Also, such assessment permits judgment about the capacity of the child to learn from experiences and to apply previous learning to new situations. In the school setting or in other learning situations, it permits grouping the children, if this is desired.

Development of Competence

During the early years, there is also the development of self-sufficiency and competence. The child shows increasing autonomy,

---

1. See Dorothy Flapan, *Children's Understanding of Social Interaction*, New York: Teachers College Press, Columbia University, 1968.

independence, purposiveness. He becomes more responsible for himself. There is an increased emphasis on mastering activities and on mastering the daily realities—for instance, learning to feed himself, toilet himself, and dress himself. As he matures, the child also becomes more capable of controlling his impulses, delaying gratifications and/or accepting substitute gratification, tolerating frustration and handling stresses, demands, and pressures.

The infant is unable to wait; he needs immediate gratification. There is low frustration tolerance and an intense reaction when he is hungry or uncomfortable or cannot do what he is trying to do. He is impulsive, grabbing things he wants and seeming to have little control over his impulses. Gradually, he develops some capacity to be diverted. He becomes increasingly able to delay gratification and to wait for a moderate amount of time without a violent reaction. Also, he becomes increasingly able to accept substitute gratifications, though he might express his disappointment or irritation.

In many ways, the child gradually becomes able to accept and adapt to the limitations of reality. He learns to tolerate moderate amounts of anxiety and develops ways of dealing with his anxiety through various emerging "defense mechanisms." He also continues to develop some capacity to control himself. During this time, the child is learning to anticipate events and the consequences of his own actions; to use judgment in deciding between various courses of action; and to plan, reason, and organize.

As can be seen, in this section we refer to a variety of ego functions—achievements, mastery, being active and achieving a certain degree of independence, achieving control of body functions, tolerating frustrations, dealing with anxiety, and becoming more reality-oriented. All of these are included here since they are what respondents often think of and refer to as "competence."

Social and Sex Identity

From about three years of age, the child shows a developing awareness of himself as a person and of his social and sex identity. He comes to recognize that he is a member of his immediate family and of his larger social group in the community, as well as a member of a specific sex group.

In the beginning, there was no differentiation of the self from others but rather a dependency on the mothering person to know and satisfy the child's wishes. Slowly, he learns to distinguish between himself and the world around him and becomes aware of himself as separate from others, trying to control them and trying not to be controlled by them. He talks about himself as a third person, and he becomes aware of his own likes and dislikes. He looks at himself and describes himself from the viewpoint of others—for example, "I am a good boy"; "I am a pretty girl."

In the chapter on social development we spoke of separation and individuation. To individuate also means to accept a certain social role assignment. This role includes the child's expected behavior within the family. It refers to the degree to which he must carry out certain functions within the family. It involves how the child sees other members of the immediate family and how he is seen by them—as good or bad, as competent or incompetent, as valued or resented. All of these factors contribute toward the child's concept of himself, his identity.

The role assignment within the family and the social identity of the family are carried into the outside world and influence how the child sees himself in relationship to other children and other families. As already referred to in chapter 3, the responses of other children and adults to the child, as well as his responses to them, will slowly bring about a wider sense of his own identity. This process goes on continually throughout childhood, and in adolescence there is a new identity consolidation and organization. Thus, the social identity develops in relation to the child's environment, which includes the immediate and extended family, the schools, other institutions in the neighborhood, and the role of the family within the larger community.

The child's identity also includes his sex identity. Today there is much information about differences between the sexes from birth, but, in addition, there is a much greater awareness of the impact of the environment in relation to sex differences.

In the beginning, within the family a child is simply *a child*, and mother and father are the child's parents, whom he sees in relationship to his needs. However, by the age of three years, after individuation has occurred, a new facet of identity has begun to develop.

Mother is identified as a *woman* and father as a *man;* and the child confronts the question, "Am I a girl or a boy?"; and, of course, the further question, "What does this mean?"

Assignment of the sex role is a complicated one and is inter-related in various ways with the social role assignment. Different social roles are assigned to boys and girls, and the environment has different expectations of a child depending on the sex role. The child gradually becomes aware that there are "sex-appropriate" behaviors that society and the family prescribe for males and for females. He tries to imitate the behaviors of the same-sex parent and begins the process of identifying with that parent.

The evolving sex identity is significant as the child establishes his role within the family and continues his developmental progression into the oedipal phase of psychic organization (which is discussed more fully in chapter 6, "Phase Development"). During the oedipal (or family integration) phase, the child relates to his parents with his newly acquired sex identity and with wishes and expectations in relation to father "as a man" and to mother "as a woman."

As with other aspects of development, there is much variation during the process of acquiring a sex identity. Some children are delayed in their sex differentiating development, while others are relatively precocious in developing a sex identity. Some easily identify with the same-sex parent, while others find it difficult. These factors in turn will significantly affect relationships within the family, as well as relationships in the larger social world, with consequences for social development, emotional development, and some aspects of ego development.

Assessment of Ego Development

Ego development is the aspect of development that has been most emphasized in the past in assessing young children because it is easily available to parents, teachers, pediatricians, day-care workers, and public-health specialists. Motor functioning and intellectual functioning are behaviors typically observed in a school situation and in the home and, in fact, have often been used by teachers in their own evaluations of children or by school psychologists in making recommendations for the children.

As with the previous aspects of development, the items selected for the assessment of ego development by means of the Short Assessment Outline are only a small proportion of what had been assessed in the comprehensive clinical study. However, when these items were combined, they offered a valid and reliable indication of the child's ego developmental status.[2]

---

2. See Appendix B for discussion of validity and reliability.

Criteria for Assessing
EGO DEVELOPMENT

Mastery

Phase	Characteristic, expected, typical	Uncharacteristic, unexpected, atypical, pathological Ranging from:	To:
Infant: birth to 1½ (Oral Phase)	In the beginning, complete dependence for physical needs and bodily care. Bodily needs dependent on outside — to be turned, moved, fed, dressed, toileted. Beginnings of mastery — turning, sitting, crawling, walking, feeding self, reaching for objects. Needs much help. Signals hunger and discomfort and desire for assistance. Beginning to distinguish between self and world around him. Handling toys, pots, stuffed animals, etc. Pushing and/or pulling toys.	More attacking than dependent (fighting against object). Strenuous efforts to become independent. Cannot accept dependency.	Delay in turning, sitting, crawling, walking. Little or no attempt to reach for objects, feed self. Extreme helplessness. Gets help by crying, appearing helpless. Great dependency.
Toddler: 1½ to 3 (Anal Phase)	Gaining control of own body — feeds self, toilets self, tries to dress self. Asserting own controls (negative phase of independency). Does what he wants and in his way. Body movements coming under control, becoming smooth. Coordination good; dexterity good. Running, climbing. Good use of materials and equipment. Uses moderate variety of them, enjoys them, is discriminating in their use. Attention span adequate in both self-	Strong insistence on doing everything himself. Cannot let self depend on others. Fear of being controlled by others if depends on them. Overcontrol of body movements; body movements hesitant, overcautious. Restricted in physical activities. Sits unusually long time. Perseveration and/or repetition of tasks. Limited in use of materials and/or equipment. Avoids certain ones while dealing exclusively with others. Little imag-	Little or no attempts to control own body — feed self, toilet self, dress self. Does not accept controls. Little control of body movements, movements awkward, clumsy. Stumbles, falls, is sluggish. Coordination poor, dexterity poor. Constantly active, cannot "sit still." Poor use of materials and/or equipment. Sloppy and/or destructive with toys. Uses them in inappropriate, careless, wasteful ways. No pleasure from "doing." Not easily

Phase	Characteristic, expected, typical	Uncharacteristic, unexpected, atypical, pathological	
		Ranging from:	To:
	originated and adult-initiated projects. Can become engrossed in what he is doing. Can give many activities attention.	ination, creativity, flexibility, freedom in their use. Overly concerned about being careful in their use. Extremely prolonged attention span.	involved. Distractible. Attention span short. Flies from one activity to another.
Differentiating Stage: 3 to 4½ (Phallic Phase)	Increasingly self-sufficient; needs little attention; most activities self-initiated; needs little help. Usually does not need to ask for help, but can ask for it when it is needed and/or after own efforts have not succeeded; can accept help. Asks for what he wants. Able to plan what he is going to do and carry out his plans. Usually "keeps trying," finishes what he begins. Functioning seems adequate for his age. Behavior organized, purposeful, yet adaptable and spontaneous. Girls more likely than boys to show inhibited mobility, more likely than boys to have good coordination, good dexterity.	*Cannot* ask for anything, because *has* to prove his strength and power to overcome his own doubts. Never asks for and usually rejects help, if help is offered. Will not accept help even when it is needed. Cannot ask for what he wants—sees it as admission of weakness. Mode of getting what he wants appears to be stereotyped, nonadaptable, unspontaneous.	Unable to carry out what he wants to do. Few techniques for getting what he wants. Becomes easily discouraged about achieving what he set out to do and quickly asks for help or just "gives up" without finishing what he started. Behavior often appears to be disorganized, purposeless and/or nonadapting. Functioning seems inept, inadequate for age. Usually afraid to "try." Needs to have much structure and firmness from adult.

Phase	Characteristic, expected, typical	Uncharacteristic, unexpected, atypical, pathological	
		Ranging from:	To:
Family Integration: 4½ to 6 (Oedipal Phase)	Usually makes active attempt to master or cope with difficult, new, or challenging situation and usually is able to cope with it. Usually has a sense of his own power; aware of his abilities and uses them freely. Often takes initiative, takes responsibility, thinks for himself, tries to solve problems. Increasingly able to handle pressure from external environment. Good adaptation to school. Willing to take some risks; has courage. Appears moderately independent, autonomous, adaptable, flexible. Mastery of materials. Girls more likely than boys to show rigidity in functioning.	*Has* to deal with situation himself. Extreme determination. Forces himself to cope with it. *Has* to take responsibility. Rebuffs encouragement, reassurance, support from others. Insists on coping with difficult, new or challenging situations himself. Even where unsuccessful in handling them himself, will not ask for help and will reject offers of help. Cannot acknowledge any shortcomings. Takes too many risks, constantly proving he has courage. Inflexible.	In difficult, new, or challenging situation, usually moves away and/or becomes passive. Usually does not try to master situation or else tries and is unable to cope with it. No sense of power. Feels helpless. Needs encouragement, reassurance, support from others to use his abilities. Seldom takes initiative; avoids or refuses responsibility. Cannot handle pressures from environment. Poor adaptation to school. Gives up easily, asks for help; discouraged. Afraid to try new things; afraid to risk.

Criteria for Assessing
EGO DEVELOPMENT

Communication

Phase	Characteristic, expected, typical	Uncharacteristic, unexpected, atypical, pathological	
		Ranging from:	To:
Infant: birth to 1½ (Oral Phase)	Communicates by crying, by noises, by body movements, by gestures; smiles. Beginning to use simple words.	Incessant efforts to communicate, often frantic — crying, screaming, agitated body movements or gestures.	Little effort to communicate, even by cries and sounds. "Quiet baby"; "You hardly know the baby is there." Delay in attempts to use words.
Toddler: 1½ to 3 (Anal Phase)	Communicates by actions, one-word sentences, simple sentences. Language used to get needs met, to tell others what to do. Monologues, much talking, verbal curiosity, inquiries.	Continuous talking — used as a way to control other people, to hold on to them. *Has* to comment on everything he is doing, everything he sees.	Inhibits communication. Little use of words. Can understand what is said and knows the words, but holds back. May be negativistic, may be fearful.
Differentiating Stage: 3 to 4½ (Phallic Phase)	Able to express himself more or less adequately in speech. Good vocabulary. Able to exchange ideas, explain to others, ask questions, express desires, describe events, exchange information. Speaks with ease. Has good pronunciation.	Talks incessantly, to "show off," to compete with others, to get attention. Able to exchange ideas, explain to others, ask questions, but does these in extremely wordy way. Overwhelms others with a "flood of words."	Unable to express himself in speech. Inhibits communication; difficulty learning vocabulary. Little ability to exchange ideas, explain to others, ask questions. May be due to speech difficulty; may be because unable to assert self, unable to compete.

Phase	Characteristic, expected, typical	Uncharacteristic, unexpected, atypical, pathological	
		Ranging from:	To:
Family Integration: 4½ to 6 (Oedipal Phase)	Communication moves from egocentric to sociocentric. Directs his language toward others and tries to influence their actions and thoughts. Learning to use language to plan activities with others and to coordinate group activities.	Communication resembles that of a younger child. Primarily egocentric. Absorbed in own words. Does not "communicate" in mutual give-and-take. Pushes others away with words.	Restricted communication. Minimally answers others. Does not initiate conversation. Limited vocabulary. Silent most of the time.

Criteria for Assessing
EGO DEVELOPMENT

Curiosity—Exploration, Thinking, Learning

Phase	Characteristic, expected, typical	Uncharacteristic, unexpected, atypical, pathological	
		Ranging from:	To:
Infant: birth to 1½ (Oral Phase)	Beginning to notice "the world," to show curiosity, to explore. Handles objects; crawls and pokes into corners, cupboards, shelves, etc. Alert; responsive to surroundings — to sight, sound, touch.	"Attacks" or "devours" the world with eyes, hands. *Has* to get into everything.	Little interest in "the world"; no explorations. Seldom manipulates things. Unresponsive to surroundings; sluggish quality. Limited awareness of things.
Toddler: 1½ to 3 (Anal Phase)	Curious about self and world. Expanding capacity to perceive world and explore it. Walks into various rooms, climbs, wanders in park; inquisitive. Shows interest and freedom to explore environment. Interest in solving problems. Thinking often unrealisitc, magical.	"Pushes" to "find out" everything. Intense curiosity about everything. Much questioning. "Gets into" everything; frequently requires restraint by others.	Capacity to perceive world and explore it is inhibited. Shows little curiosity or freedom to explore. Inhibits curiosity about and interest in self and/or world. Any explorations are frightening, brief, erratic.
Differentiating Stage: 3 to 4½ (Phallic Phase)	Beginning to learn simple concepts of distance (space), time, number. Interest in learning. Some progress in learning — is about where he is expected to be for his chronological age. Expresses and shows curiosity about differences between boys and girls, about differences between children and adults. Development from magical thinking to more realistic thinking. In contact with reality, though some	Great and intense interest in learning. Continual questioning, searching for answers. Great and intense curiosity about differences between boys and girls, about differences between children and adults. "Bound" by reality; does not permit himself to engage in fantasy.	Confusion about basic concepts of distance, time, number. Inhibits any interest in learning or in intellectual functioning. May be resistant to learning situations; may avoid learning situations. Little progress in learning — is behind what is expected for his chronological age.

Phase	Characteristic, expected, typical	Uncharacteristic, unexpected, atypical, pathological	
		Ranging from:	To:
	fantasy. Able to maintain contact with reality and to interpret reality correctly. Better able than previously to differentiate between fantasy and reality.		Frequent and prolonged periods of time spent in fantasy. Difficulty interpreting reality; difficulty differentiating between fantasy and reality.
Family Integration: 4½ to 6 (Oedipal Phase)	Seems to realize his own potentialities in school and at home. Pleasure in intellectual functioning. Expansiveness; curiosity, freedom in exploring. Can anticipate, use judgment, plan, reason, organize, synthesize. Moving from concrete to abstract thinking; from perception to conception to explanation to inference and interpretation. Developing creativity in the use of materials and/or equipment. Improving in making judgments and in decision-making.	"Strains" to function beyond potentialities. Pushes self. "Overachiever." Little creativity in the use of materials and/or equipment.	Intellectual functioning does not seem to be up to child's potentialities. Learning difficulties; learning "blocks"; difficult to teach. "Underachiever." "Poor in making judgments and/or in decision-making.

Criteria for Assessing
EGO DEVELOPMENT

Delay of Gratification; Frustration Tolerance; Impulse Control

Phase	Characteristic, expected, typical	Uncharacteristic, unexpected, atypical, pathological	
		Ranging from:	To:
Infant: birth to 1½ (Oral Phase)	First half year, unable to wait; needs immediate gratification. Low frustration tolerance. Intense reaction when hungry, uncomfortable, not given what he wants. Deprivation elicits aggressive response. Impulsive - grab what he wants. Little or no control over impulses.	Cannot wait even a short time. No frustration tolerance. Any delay or frustration is intolerable and he becomes frantic.	Waits without reaction of displeasure. "Takes" delay and/or frustration without reacting as expected. Mild indication of hunger, discomfort, but then appears to resign himself.
	One-half to one-and-a-half, gradually develops capacity for delay and capacity to be diverted. Accepts schedule. Develops some control over impulses. As he feels assured satisfaction will follow, he shows capacity for increasing delay of gratification.	No capacity for substitute gratification; no capacity to be diverted. Cannot accept routines, schedules. No control over impulses.	
Toddler: 1½ to 3 (Anal Phase)	Able to wait a moderate length of time for gratification. Also, increasing capacity for substitute gratification and increasing capacity to be diverted. Moderate frustration tolerance when he is not given what he wants or cannot do what he is trying to do.	Immediate, intense reaction to any frustration or interference with desires.

Reacts as if still in oral phase. | Inhibition of impulses. Cannot act impulsively at any time. Appears to have extreme frustration tolerance. Inhibits overt expressions of frustration. Gives impression of great patience. |
| | Increasing control over impulses, though still some impulsivity. Increasing capacity to delay gratifi- | | |

Phase	Characteristic, expected, typical	Uncharacteristic, unexpected, atypical, pathological	
		Ranging from:	To:
	cation and/or accept substitute gratification — though he may express his disappointment and irritation. Increasingly able to accept limitations of reality and postponement of gratification.		
Differentiating Stage: 3 to 4½ (Phallic Phase)	Able to tolerate anxiety and has "defense mechanisms" against anxiety.	Reacts as if still in oral or anal phase (see above).	Reacts as if still in oral or anal phase (see above).
Family Integration: 4½ to 6 (Oedipal Phase)	Shows control over impulses. Can tolerate "average" delays of gratification, can accept substitute gratification at times. Able to tolerate moderate amounts of frustration as part of daily living.	Reacts as if still in oral or anal phase (see above).	Reacts as if still in oral or anal phase (see above).

Criteria for Assessing
EGO DEVELOPMENT

Social & Sex Identification

Phase	Characteristic, expected, typical	Uncharacteristic, unexpected, atypical, pathological	
		Ranging from:	To:
Infant: birth to 1½ (Oral Phase)	No clear differentiation of self. Feels mother (or mother-substitute) should be able to "read his mind"; world should know his wishes. Sense of identity is poor and fluid. Beginning to distinguish between self and world around him—respond to surroundings (sounds, sights); reach out for and handle what is seen.		
Toddler: 1½ to 3 (Anal Phase)	Aware of self as separate from others — trying to control others and/or trying not to be controlled by others. May talk about self as a third person. Aware of some of own wants, likes and dislikes. Looks at and describes self from viewpoint of others, eg., "good boy."		
Differentiating Stage: Boy 3 to 4½ (Phallic Phase)	Indications of identification of self as a boy — aware of sex-appropriate behaviors for a boy (e.g., more aggressive than girls in play and fantasy; more likely than girls to use overt conflict, with hitting, shoving, wrestling); prefers activities and objects defined as appropriate for boys (e.g., guns).	Exaggerated masculinity — almost caricature of stereotype of "boy." Has to reject any behaviors, interests, activities which might be considered "for girls."	Confusion re sexual identification; may identify with opposite sex; may slip from one sex to the other.

Phase	Characteristic, expected, typical	Uncharacteristic, unexpected, atypical, pathological	
		Ranging from:	To:
Differentiating Stage: Girl 3 to 4½ (Phallic Phase)	Indications of identification of self as a girl — aware of sex-appropriate behaviors for a girl (e.g., less aggressive than boys in play and fantasy; somewhat passive and dependent; more likely than boys to use verbal conflict rather than physical conflict); prefers activities and objects defined as appropriate for girls (e.g., cooking, jewelry).	Exaggerated feminity — almost caricatures stereotype of "girl." *Has* to reject any behaviors, interests, activities which might be considered "for boys."	Confusion re sexual identification; may identify with opposite sex; may slip from one sex to the other.
Family Integration: 4½ to 6 (Oedipal Phase)	Recognizes self as a member of his family and of his social group in the community. Boy identifies with and imitates father, e.g., in walk, mannerisms, voice, facial expressions, interests; girl identifies with and imitates mother.	Boy avoids father, wants to be different from father; imitates mother; doesn't like to play with other boys; doesn't like "masculine" activities; walks and talks like a girl. Girl avoids mother, wants to be different from mother, imitates father; doesn't like to play with girls; doesn't like "feminine" activities; walks and talks like a boy.	Does not recognize that he is a member of his family—rejects family, "searches" for a family to belong to. Cannot identify with father or mother: seeks someone to identify with.

Chapter 6
Phase Development

The way a child proceeds in his general developmental unfolding is another indication of his progression in development. Within the psychoanalytic developmental framework, the child is conceived of as passing through several phases in the course of his development from infancy to latency (which was the phase at which our study terminated)—an oral, anal, phallic, and oedipal phase. In each phase, he shows certain developmental landmarks and phase-appropriate behaviors. Each phase is characterized by certain pleasure-seeking strivings and certain assertive-aggressive strivings, which extract from the outside world the satisfaction of the individual's needs; and each phase has its own tasks and its own masteries, as well as its own concerns, needs, and conflicts.

It is expected that there will be progression in the expression of the libidinal and aggressive drives—the child learning to delay the expression of aggression and to express his aggression in ways acceptable to his family, peer group and community. There is movement toward fusing mastery of the environment with satisfaction of the individual's desires for pleasure and assertion.

Inferences can be made about progression in the libidinal and aggressive drives by evaluating evidences of the needs which dominate the child, the conflicts he encounters and masters, his concerns and anxieties, the inhibition-expression of the libidinal and aggressive drives, and the libidinal-aggressive balance.

Libidinal Phases

Each phase of development is represented by a central theme. The pleasures-gratifications of the child, his play and other activities, his character traits, and the symptoms that appear are related to this theme. Thus, getting information about these areas and inferring the child's anxieties and conflicts can suggest the level of development the child has reached. Such information would include observations about the child's eating, sleeping and toileting habits, interest in various parts of his body, problem behavior, assertive-aggressive and affectionate behaviors, and his reactions to the assertive-aggressive and affectionate behaviors of others.

Proposing that there are phases of development implies that in each period there is a specific psychic organization, followed by a new emerging phase with psychic reorganization. In each phase there are "appropriate" conflicts which are resolved and which subsequently have an impact on the reorganization of the phase. There is, therefore, the assumption that phases proceed according to a certain hierarchy and that each succeeding phase of development takes over and supersedes the earlier phase. Usually we assume that the earlier phase is sufficiently reorganized so that a discontinuity is implied; as the later phase takes over, problems of the earlier phase recede into the background or disappear.

It is, then, clear that when the problem or conflict is not resolved within one phase, this can interfere with the emergence of the next phase and the new psychic organization cannot supersede the earlier phase. Also, we find there are children who enter a succeeding phase of development but are unable to face the new problems and then retreat to an earlier phase of organization. Thus, we may see the momentum of phase progression or phase regression in the face of undue circumstances which do not support the child enough in his progressive pull.

Although in this chapter we are speaking about *libidinal* phases of development, they are obviously coordinated with ego and aggressive strivings. However, the striving toward gratification of a libidinal nature or the pleasure of achievement, of novelty, and of newness in relationships has a primary position in developmental organization.

Important considerations in assessing the child's libidinal development are the pleasures and gratifications he seeks in each phase, the exaggerations of these, or the absence of what is expected in the phase. Certain manifestations are associated with the oral phase, others with the anal, phallic, or oedipal phases. The child's inability to accept the implications of each successive phase may result in distortions in the emerging behaviors in each phase of development. Thus, symptoms can be interpreted as ways of handling anxiety or as inappropriate conflict solutions.

In this chapter we have tried to present the expected observable behaviors of the child in each phase of development. Since the concept of libidinal phases is based on theoretical propositions, in our study we looked for the manifestations as expressed in the overt behavior. We realized that by doing this we were thereby missing the child's fantasies, his inner experiences, and his motivations. Nevertheless, we are convinced that what can be observed and studied, particularly by persons who are familiar with this age group and who have regular contact with it, provides sufficient information to be used to judge each developmental phase.

Infant: Birth to One-and-a-Half Years (Oral Phase)

Pleasures-Gratifications. During infancy and for some time after, stimulation of the mouth is most pleasurable—hence, the word *oral*. The infant has the need for immediate gratification and tension reduction, and his tension is reduced mainly through the mouth—sucking, swallowing, and exploring. Gratification is in the context of a nurturing, dependent relationship with "mother" or a mother surrogate. There is pleasure in eating, and the infant is expected to have a good appetite and good digestion. He has pleasure in sucking and becomes increasingly able to give himself gratification by thumb- or finger-sucking or sucking other objects. He also finds pleasure in mouthing or oral exploring and eventually in biting and chewing.

Although oral activities are most pleasurable for the infant, during this phase he also finds pleasure in body contact and body care—being held, cuddled, stroked, handled. There is pleasure in his own body functioning; there is pleasure in the use of his musculature—

first the movements of his body, arms, or legs and later the movements in turning, sitting, crawling, walking, and rhythmical movements such as rocking or swaying. There is also pleasure from the natural rhythm of sleeping-waking. (Simultaneously, there are expressions of emerging ego functions.)

Theme. The basic theme of the oral phase is need-gratification. Especially during the first half-year of life, the child is in a condition in which need-gratification is most outstanding. By *need* we refer to those factors which impose upon the outside world to care for the child and provide gratification for him. Later on there is much more expression of the ego function and the direct influence of psychic drive expressions.

The "mother" is seen as need-gratifying and tension-reducing, and her presence is linked with gratification and with protection against internal tension. The characteristic anxiety of the very young child, therefore, revolves around the loss of the "mother," the caretaking person. There is anxiety about being abandoned, being deprived. On a preverbal level, the infant's concerns are, "Will I be cared for or neglected?" "Will I get satisfaction or deprivation?" "Will there be constancy of the mother's care or loss of it?" "Will there be a rhythm of tension-and-release or will there be chronic, unrelieved tension?" According to Erikson, it is during this phase that basic trust is developed.

Play. In his play, a child may elaborate on his current anxieties, concerns, and conflicts and may express his impulses. Thus, the infant may engage in "oral" play, pretending that he is being fed, making food or giving food to someone else, or even feeding a baby. There may be play at biting others or devouring others or fears of being bitten or devoured. There may be play that food is taken away and brought back or that people or things will be "lost" and then found. At this age, peek-a-boo is a favorite activity, as is dropping an object and having someone else retrieve it.

During this phase, there is an emergence of the anticipation of events and some fantasy expression. The child has learned to be comfortable with the known but turns away from the unknown — thus, the smile for someone recognized and the fear reaction to strangers.

Character Traits. Character traits are a result of the drive discharge, the child's defense against anxiety aroused by the drive, and the child's mode of relating to others. The character traits are the relatively fixed ways of relating to the world and to other people. Thus, if we observe a child's behaviors with others, we can determine his characteristic style, those actions which have become a part of his character and therefore have become stable and are continuous. Examining the child's characteristic ways of relating to others permits us to see the child's phase-appropriate concerns and his conflicts and those forms of behavior which are drive-determined. From these an inference can be made about his developmental status.

The newborn infant is dependent on others for his physical and emotional needs but he gradually becomes more independent. In order to let the outside world know about his needs, he gives non-verbal as well as preverbal signals, and he depends on the mother to "read" these signals and to respond to them appropriately. The world in which the infant exists is one of egocentricity. While physically separated from the mother at birth, emotionally there is a long period in which the "hatching" has to occur. Thus, while the child feels in contact with the outside world, he feels that the outside world is part of him; and if separation does occur between him and the outside world, he assumes that the outside world's function is connected only with him. This is his egocentricity. He gradually learns to respond to the outside world, particularly the mother. However, even though there is a very fine early orchestration between mother and child, we assume that this interaction system takes place without recognition of the mother as an independent person with her own feelings and needs.

The infant is receptive to what is given to him and may be compliant as a way of getting his needs met. He is trusting in the expectation that his needs *will* be met and that he will be cared for. If, however, he experiences prolonged tension and the caretaking person is not there, the child may become overwhelmed with anxiety.

Traits such as dependence, receptivity, compliance, demandingness, and attempting to get from the environment whatever is needed are characteristic of the oral phase. They may, however, continue long beyond infancy. An "oral" child may "give up easily" and look to others in a helpless way to be symbolically "fed," or he may be forever demanding. Other indications of concern about being cared for include clinging behavior and efforts to please others. On the other hand, incorporating, devouring, and engulfing expectations or fears are also considered "oral," since they are associated with this phase. Such a child may seem difficult to satisfy and may seem to complain about whatever he is given.

Symptoms. The child's direct oral expressions, as well as the exaggerations of these or the denial or absence of them, may suggest the child's phase conflicts. For example, a child may be a finicky eater or an overeater; he may have extreme food preferences or avoidances; he may indulge in excessive sucking (finger, thumb, or other objects), biting, cheweing, or oral exploring. Other children may give the impression of insatiability, with complaints about not getting enough (food, attention, gifts) or not being treated fairly.

Or, in contrast to the preceding, in cases where the mother has not met the needs of the child, the child may "turn away" from mother and may appear precociously independent or may "turn to" others as substitutes for mother—adults such as father or teacher.

The child's sleeping and resting habits should also be noted. If the child is often wakeful or too agitated to rest, it may be indicative of some anxiety. Exaggerations of "oral" character traits and/or repetitive "oral" play may also be considered symptoms, to be investigated further.

Progression to the Next Phase. Although a child may still show oral manifestations or character traits, any one of these alone does not indicate the level of a child's developmental progression. It should be noted that the same symptoms or the same behavior may have many different meanings. They may, in fact, have different meanings for a given child at different times in his life. For example, during the oral phase, thumb-sucking may be a substitute for mother's breast or for the bottle, and it may be a normal expression of the child's function. In the next phase, however, there may be thumb-sucking; and while the overt behavior is the same, the meaning of it for the child may be different. It may still be what it was in the first year-and-a-half of life—a substitute for mother's body and food. But it may now mean that the child uses thumb-sucking as a function of "his" body controls, of doing it his own way. Or the child may experiment with mastery of body function to prove that his actions are under his own control rather than dependent on some outside person. Thus, the same behavior may have a different meaning in each phase.

Any specific behavior or characteristic of a child must be evaluated in its relation to the overall developmental phase organization and to the inner experience of the child.

Toddler: One-and-a-Half to Three Years (Anal Phase)

Pleasure-Gratifications. Following the oral phase, the next phase of development focuses on the task of acquiring control of the child's body functions. The word *anal* refers to the capacity of the child to take over the control of his own body. Toilet training is part of the interaction with the mother. The mother directs where the toileting takes place, she determines the timing of it, and the child's function of toileting is a part of the emotional and verbal interplay with the mother. Thus, the child does not just experience his body as if it were independent from the environment but experiences it in response to the environment and the influence which the environment has on it. Children will be proud to show mother that they can use the potty successfully, or that they finished their bowel movement; and the mother will praise the child for it. In this way, the body controls are seen as part of a very significant social experience.

During the anal phase, the child is interested in toileting in general, his own and that of others, and may show interest in looking at or touching his bowel movements. He is also interested in his own buttocks and those of others.

It is during this period that the child accepts a certain orderliness in what is being done. He becomes interested in schedules and learns to accept scheduled times for toileting, meals, and going to bed. The parents and child may set up specific routines for these activities and therefore create certain ways of performing an activity repetitively. This obviously leads to the establishment of rituals. To achieve control over his whole body function, the child makes efforts to be clean, punctual, and orderly. This is also the period when there is pleasure in acquiring control of other musculature—large muscles for climbing and running, small muscles for handling objects.

Theme. The basic theme of the anal phase is body control and the evolvement of a control system. It can be stated by concerns such as, "Can I exercise control over myself *and* my environment, or will I *be* controlled by others and/or by environmental factors?" "Can I control myself or will I *lose* control?" The theme of control as against loss of control is related to that of omnipotence/helplessness. Related to this, there are also the themes of keeping or losing, keeping or giving away, and possession or loss of possession.

Associated with his training to "be on schedule" and to follow emerging rituals, there may be concern about being dirty or clean or disorderly or orderly.

A new autonomy is being acquired by the child exercising the right to say, "No," to push the mother away. However, if the child asserts himself, there is the risk that he will have to "pay the consequences." Thus, there is concern about getting hurt and hurting, being destroyed and destroying.

Negativism is the normal expression of the child attempting to achieve his individuality. It seems that one does not find one's own "I" or one's own way of doing things when one does it only in concert and in harmony with others. When done *against* others, in differentiation from others, it seems to gain significance. This is characteristic of the anal phase (and later on again in adolescence when individuality is achieved in opposition to the environment for a transitional period of time). Therefore, the negativism of the child during the anal period is part of his normal way of establishing differentiation. Opposition means, "I do it my way. If I do it your way, then I don't decide what is to be done."

The characteristic anxieties during the anal phase are the fear of loss of control and fear of the loss of mother's love. As previously noted, during the oral phase there is the fear of losing the caretaking person. But as the child reaches the anal phase, this is changed to the fear of losing the affection and love of the mother. This is a very significant step.

During the anal phase, the possessiveness, "It's mine and not yours," brings about a differentiation between outside, "yours," and "mine." The child differentiates himself from the outside world and recognizes what is his and what is not his.

Play. Children in the anal phase may play at toileting or have dolls play at toileting, soiling, and messing. In their play, children may express feelings about being dirty or clean, organized or disorganized, orderly or disorderly. "Anal" play may be disorganized and impulsive or the opposite—neat, organized, and repetitive.

"Bathroom" talk is common during this phase; and children may giggle and call each other names such as "Boo-boo," "Poo-poo," or "Dooty." Play with sand, clay, dirt, and paint are popular.

There may be repetitiveness in building something and destroying it. At times, children may "collect" and guard particular toys and equipment. In playing, a child may have dolls hurt one another in various ways.

Also, during the anal phase, there is an outburst of pleasure in exploring the environment as part of the child's learning and desire to control.

Character Traits. The character traits are an expression of the various concerns and conflicts of the child during the anal phase. These become built into the developmental reorganization. As the child is making efforts to control himself and to do this on schedule, his efforts are directed toward being clean, punctual, and orderly. Traits such as extreme orderliness or disorderliness, cleanliness or dirtiness, and punctuality or lack of punctuality may therefore become a part of his character if he does not appropriately resolve these conflicts.

There is emphasis on "my" and "mine," and the trait of possessiveness may appear. As he is making efforts to protect himself against being controlled by others, he may characteristically act defiant, obstinate, quarrelsome. Because he wants to "do it himself"—in his own way and at his own time—there is negativism. It is as if the child were saying, "I will do what I want when I want." This position may then become part of his character. The struggle which is expressed in negativism can become part of the character. He may stay in an oppositional attitude to the world, so that whatever the world does he considers inappropriate or has doubts about and has to oppose. On the other hand, if the child's normal negativism is not lived through and he is not permitted to assert his individuality, it may lead with other factors to his becoming one who submits, overaccepts, or acts overfriendly.

The "anal" child is reluctant to give up on demand what he has or produces, and yet he may take pleasure in deciding himself to "give" a gift of what is his or what he has "produced." Characteristically, there may, therefore, be hoarding and stinginess or extravagance and wastefulness.

In his attempts to control others, the child may often show bossiness and domination. Or, because of the concern about his own aggression and that of others (discussed in more detail later) and his concern about his own and others' destructiveness, as well as his concern about losing the love of his mother if he does not accept her control, there may be ambivalence.

Symptoms. When the inherent drive to control one's own body is interfered with, this may lead to pathological symptoms. Then, instead of efforts toward growth, there are efforts toward denying the drive or toward working through the fears through excessive, exaggerated forms of activity. The fears and conflicts about control issues may overwhelm or interfere with further development and create compulsive or obsessive features as the phase-specific tasks remain unresolved.

Distortions in behavior related to body functions—such as, constipation, diarrhea, soiling, and bed-wetting—as well as rituals, compulsions, or obsessions may be emerging symptoms and may indicate the child's conflicts.

Progression to the Next Phase. Though one may observe anal behaviors or anal characteristics at later stages, these alone do not necessarily indicate that the child is still on an anal level of development. As stated in the discussion of the oral phase of development, it is possible that not all of the conflicts will be appropriately resolved at a specific phase. There is overlapping from one phase to another, and therefore we may see symptoms from the anal phase carried into the next phase. However, often these carried-over conflicts may gain new meanings. Thus, we must again emphasize that the same behavior which had one meaning at the anal stage may have a different meaning in the next phase. For example, while orderliness or cleanliness or body concerns may appear to be anal in nature, they may take on a phallic meaning for the child. Or, again using the example of thumb-sucking given in the section on oral manifestations, what was oral could acquire an anal meaning of control over one's own body and then during the next phase be linked to phallic characteristics—namely, body integrity, body injuries, or the feeling of power. Thus, behaviors or characteristics initially associated with the anal phase must be examined in relation to the overall organization of the child's development at each stage.

Differentiating Stage: Three to Four-and-a-Half Years (Phallic Phase)

Pleasures-Gratifications. During the phallic phase, the child reaches a developmental organization centered around his role differentiation. He has established a sufficiently secure relationship with the people in his environment to achieve object constancy, so that he can now be secure enough *with* himself and *by* himself. He has differentiated himself from the environment, at least to the degree that he is controlling his own body functions. His new task is to find the role assignment of the newly found "I" in relationship with the "You." The child wishes to be big and powerful, strong and invulnerable. At the same time, he is afraid that he is small and vulnerable. He is afraid that his body integrity is not too secure, and he tends to compensate for his unsureness with a magic belief in his power. The phallic child gets pleasure from being admired and from the attention and praise he receives. He enjoys "showing off" his abilities, achievements, and attractiveness. As part of assessing and confirming his own development, he enjoys comparing himself with others—to see who is taller, faster, stronger, etc.

There is then the task of establishing his sex identity. Boys and girls become interested in their sex roles and will explore the meaning of this. On a cognitive level they want to understand the differences between boys and girls in their roles and the differences in their bodies. There is interest in exhibiting and exploring one's own body, as well as in looking at and exploring the bodies of others. The boy becomes aware of his masculinity and the girl of her femininity. Both are curious about the parental roles. The father becomes the male whom the boy imitates and with whom he identifies, while the mother becomes the female whom the girl imitates and with whom she identifies.

Theme. The basic themes of the phallic phase focus on, "Who am I as a boy or as a girl?" There is concern about self-worth as it is related to sex differentiation and identification. Also, there is concern whether one is admired or ridiculed and whether one is bigger or smaller, stronger or weaker than others. With the evolving sex identity and recognition of the sex differences, there is anxiety which revolves around body damage and injury—castration fear.

Play. At the phallic phase, the child engages in much active, thrusting activity. Phallic children compete for attention and praise and for equipment and materials. There is fun in water play and carpentry, sawing wood and building. Materials are used in a constructive way, and there is much emphasis on skills and on mastery in activity.

Also, there is simple dramatic play—the children playing real and unreal social roles, such as doctor, teacher, ballerina, monster, superman, and wonder woman. But, in addition, they enjoy the process of just "dressing up" as the adults in their immediate environment.

There is much curiosity about human anatomy and talk about the differences between males and females. Children play the game of "show," which involves exposing the body to other children or urinating in front of them. There is also much other investigative play, taking things apart to see what is inside them and how they work.

Character Traits. One of the character traits emerging from the phallic phase is being competitive—being best, biggest, strongest, prettiest, most loved, most admired. Another "phallic" trait is being exhibitionistic—admiring oneself, bragging-boasting, "showing off." And yet another trait is being assertive and forceful. The phallic child actively seeks attention, takes pride in his accomplishments, and wants praise for his performances. The phallic boy "tries on" being "masculine" and the phallic girl being "feminine."

Symptoms. Extremes of any of these behaviors or traits or the absence of the expected behaviors and interests would suggest conflicts in the child and could lead to symptoms. An intense need to be powerful, to be admired, to exhibit or to assert is connected with underlying conflicts about not being accepted, not being admired, not being strong. The symptoms, therefore, are an expression of unresolved conflicts beyond the child's capacity to cope.

There may be excessive exhibitionism (and clowning as a derivative of exhibitionism) to reassure oneself; or intense shame or modesty about one's own body and extreme shyness as a reaction formation against exhibitionism. There also may be excessive masturbation or repression of pleasure in, and avoidance of, touching parts of one's own body.

We may find intense interest in and prolonged attention to boy-girl differences and excessive looking at the bodies of others or, at the other extreme, complete avoidance of looking. Boys may deny their masculinity or may idealize masculinity, and girls may deny their femininity or idealize femininity. Because of their doubts or conflicts, the children may constantly seek attention and praise—to the point of making themselves nuisances to others. Or, there may be the opposite trait—not daring to assert themselves and an avoidance of seeking attention, with extreme reserve and shyness.

During this period, we find symptoms such as excessive fear of injuries or other bodily harm. There may also be intense fears of doctors, dogs or other animals, thunder, or heights; and these fears may become phobias. And yet another symptom in the phallic phase is the emergence of nightmares.

The avoidance of phallic play and the usual, expected activities of "phallic" children might also be regarded as symptomatic.

Progression to the Next Phase. A child may show phallic manifestations and characteristics, but, as noted previously, any of these alone may not necessarily indicate the level of his developmental organization. Though certain activities, interests, and behaviors are generally associated with this phase, any one of these must be examined in relation to the total developmental progression.

Family Integration: Four-and-a-Half to Six Years (Oedipal Phase)

After the child has achieved sex identity—that is, *he* is a boy and *she* is a girl, with father recognized as a man and mother as a woman—the child has to take the next step of integrating the new identity within the context of the family picture. This is the oedipal constellation. There is then both the need to identify with the same-sex parent (as there had been in the phallic phase) and at the same time the need to establish a special alliance with the opposite-sex parent. This leads to conflicts and to the working-through of the child's relationships with both parents. As a consequence, the child establishes a sense of guilt for wishes and needs that are inappropriate and that do not take into account the rights of others, including mother's and father's roles with each other. Therefore, during the oedipal phase much conflict may be expressed in fears, nightmares, and sleep disorders.

Pleasures-Gratifications. During the oedipal phase, the child experiences pleasure in identifying with the same-sex parent in likes and dislikes, mannerisms, physical movements, and physical activities. At the same time, he enjoys contact with the opposite-sex parent, with whom he flirts and whom he tries to win over as an ally. The child in the oedipal phase finds much pleasure also in achieving, in solving problems, and in mastering difficulties.

Theme. The basic theme of the oedipal phase is the romance with the opposite-sex parent. At the same time, the child is concerned about being like the same-sex parent and yet competing with that parent for the opposite-sex parent. This may cause anticipation of punishment and a significant sense of guilt for wishes which are considered "wrong" and unfair to others. There are opposing wishes which cannot easily be reconciled. The child after all is still dependent on his parents, and, while he is jealous, he nevertheless wishes to get acceptance and approval from both parents. Thus, in his emerging sex and social identity, he has to learn to control his wishes in the context of social integration and social consideration.

Because of the child's concerns about competing with the same-sex parent and possibly even replacing him in the relationship with the opposite-sex parent, the themes of the oedipal phase focus on succeeding or not daring to succeed, loving the same-sex parent and being like him or wanting to get rid of him.

Play. During the oedipal phase, the child spends much time in family play—"playing house." The boy usually plays "father" and the girl "Mother," but not always. At this age, family roles are easily shifted, even from one moment to the next.

The child is interested in the relationship between mother and father, though at times he may object to his parents being together. He has pleasure in doing things together with the same-sex parent and pleasure in playing with the opposite-sex parent. There are questions about marriage and about where babies come from and how babies are born, and there is interest about the primal scene. There may be questions about the childhood of the parents. At times children may request a baby brother or a baby sister or express a wish to have their own babies when they grow up.

Though questions about sex differences and babies have been raised earlier, at this time the same questions have a different significance. Continuing from the phallic phase, there may be sex play with other children, with much looking at one another and touching.

During the oedipal phase, children often engage in complex dramatic play in small groups and show beginning interest in small-group games. In this phase also they are beginning to explore life outside the family and to learn more about their neighborhood and the larger community, and they show a desire to visit "new" places, talk to people, and see sights.

Character Traits. The oedipal child usually becomes cooperative, friendly, and responsive. He is charming and appealing, and often is seductive, flirtatious, and even manipulative. At the same time, he is competitive with the same sex, but also appeasing, and may alternate between competing and appeasing.

Symptoms. If the child is unable to face the oedipal conflicts, he may regress to earlier phases of development. Conflicts which had been normal in the earlier phases may now become a symptom. For instance, bed-wetting may have been mastered and training in other areas may have been achieved, but during this phase returning to such behaviors will be seen as symptoms. If the oedipal desires and fantasies become too intense, they may lead to fears which force the child to retreat to earlier stages of development.

During this period one may observe sex confusion; the child may hate the same-sex parent or the opposite-sex parent. Indications of the conflicts of the oedipal phase would include that the

child act in such a way as not to identify with the same-sex parent
and to emphasize the differences from the same-sex parent or act in
such a way that he exerts great effort to appear better than the same-
sex parent. The child may avoid the opposite-sex parent because of
the "danger" of being involved with that parent. And, related to this,
he may be inhibited in displaying any hint of flirtatiousness or seductiveness wtih the opposite-sex parent, fearing the consequences if
he competes with the same-sex parent and succeeds in replacing
that parent or in defeating him. The boy may wish to be a girl in
order to appease the mother or the father, or the girl may wish to be
a boy.

There may be excessive guilt during the oedipal phase because
of the child's incestuous wishes and his wishes to eliminate the other
parent. The child may show excessive fear of either parent or of
males or females generally. As a reaction to his destructive wishes,
he may again have separation problems. Or, as noted earlier, his
fears of punishment and sense of guilt may be expressed in increasing nightmares, fears, and restlessness. The characteristic dreams
(nightmares) of this period are that the child is in danger, and he
wakes up before he is totally destroyed.

It is symptomatic if the child avoids and rebuffs the opposite-sex
parent, if the child is self-defeating in his relations with the opposite-
sex parent, or if there is exaggerated seductiveness with the
opposite-sex parent. It is also symptomatic if the child is constantly
challenging and then appeasing the same-sex parent.

The expected outcome is for the child to negotiate the oedipal phase in such a way that he does not strongly antagonize
either parent or submit too much to either one. Thus, intense antag-
onism with either parent or extreme submissiveness would also be
symptomatic.

Libidinal Phases in the Assessment Outline

Even though the libidinal component of phase development is
a theoretical formulation and can only be inferred, behaviors related
to each of the phases are available for observation and can be noted
by adults who are in regular contact with children. From these

behaviors, an estimate can then be made as to the child's progression in phase development.

The specific items included in the Short Assessment Outline which refer to the libidinal phases of development were extracted from what had been included in the comprehensive clinical study. These items, taken together and in the context of the other aspects of development, give an assessment of the child similar to that which can be obtained by doing an extensive clinical study.[1]

Aggressive Drive

In addition to the progression of the libidinal phases, it is assumed within the psychoanalytic theory that there is progression in the aggressive drive expressions. The aggressive strivings are clearly seen when they lead to destructiveness. However, aggressive strivings are part of everyday, normal functioning, and the assertive-aggressive strivings fuse with the pleasure-seeking strivings. There is change from uncontrolled aggression to aggression within bounds, which is then manifested both verbally and in actions in ways acceptable to the child's family and community.

Infant: Birth to One-and-a-Half Years (Oral Phase)

During the *oral phase* of development, the infant reveals his aggression by expressing his wants, making demands, imposing himself on his world, grabbing, devouring, and biting. There is not consideration for others; we do not expect it at this early age. The infant reacts to restraint, delay of gratification, inhibition of his activity, or to the aggression of others by crying, striking out, or increasing demandingness.

Toddler: One-and-a-Half to Three Years (Anal Phase)

Similarly, in the *anal phase* of development, the aggression of the child is seen in the ways in which he imposes his needs and wishes on the environment and on his body. We see intensification

1. See Appendix B for discussion of validity and reliability.

in his assertive-aggressive strivings during the anal phase. He energetically goes after what he wants and tries to reach his goals. He can usually control his aggression to some extent, though occasionally he "loses control."

Control over himself is connected with his wish to control others. His aggression tends to shape the environment to his desires. While he may try to control others, his reaction to the aggression of others is immediate. He attacks with language, such as scolding or criticizing others; he may shove others, hit, or get into a tug-of-war; or he may just cry (particularly in relation with siblings).

During the anal stage, the child has difficulties with impulse control. Since there is little external control of his own aggression, he must rely on external controls and on external support. His fear of punishment, and of loss of love, and also the developing fear of bodily injury, resulting in the aggression becoming modulated. However, throughout this phase, the child experiences much ambivalence and swings between "love" and "hate" for mother and other members of the family.

Differentiating Stage: Three to Four-and-a-Half Years (Phallic Phase)

During the *phallic phase* of development, the child has somewhat modulated the expression of aggression and is able to express his assertive-aggressive strivings more moderately and in more socially acceptable ways. He asserts himself when it is appropriate and pursues his own needs. He competes with other children for materials, favors, and attention. Often he competes with others through exaggeration and boasting. At times the aggression is reality bound and may be seen in achievement strivings.

In our society, girls are more likely than boys to restrain their aggressive impulses in an effort to please mother and meet mother's demands for what is considered "proper" for little girls. Yet, if there is massive inhibition of aggression and a turning of this aggression against the self, a child may develop masochistic tendencies or exhibit reactions of sadness and depression.

By the time children are in nursery school, there is usually more social use of the aggressive drive. It may be channeled into expressions acceptable to the peer group—poking, pushing, tickling, verbal provocation, or laughing. Occasionally, however, there may be strong outbursts of destructive tendencies—toward "bad" things, toward children who have failed to share desired toys or materials, or toward others who have attacked first.

At the same time, the child in the phallic phase is able to express affection easily, both verbally and through action, and to respond to the expressions of affection by others. Also, as noted in earlier chapters, he is beginning to develop the capacity for sympathy and empathy.

Family Integration: Four-and-a-Half to Six Years (Oedipal Phase)

During the *oedipal phase* of development, the child tries to achieve more satisfying relations with others and still get what he wants. The assertive-aggressive strivings are exhibited in a show of initiative, in competitiveness, in efforts to develop his own autonomy and individuality, or in attempts to master the environment.

In this phase the child wants to be competitive with the parent of the same sex. The girl will feel that she can do much better than mother and that she is able to give more understanding to father. The boy wants to be much bigger and taller and stronger than father, and at the same time he attributes superpower to his father and is afraid of this power or allies himself with it. Therefore, there is a continuous shift of the assertive strivings, which deal with replacement, identification, and competition. By the time he reaches this phase, the child can be helpful to others and may evidence altruism.

The response of the oedipal child to aggression by others is increasingly verbal and decreasingly physical. There may be insistence on compromise and mutual adjustments. In our culture, however, it appears that girls are more likely than boys to be peacemakers and compromisers.

Assessment of Aggression

An observer can note how much aggression is expressed by the child and in what ways—for example, whether it is expressed primarily in activity or in fantasy, whether there is spontaneous expression or expression only in reaction to someone else's aggression. It has been found that children who are able to show affection and friendly behaviors are also the ones who are more likely to be able to show aggressive behaviors as well.[2] Thus, an observer can see whether the child is able to express affection to others, his ways of expressing positive feelings, and how he responds to the show of affection by others.

Some children are unable to show appropriate aggression and therefore may be unable to pursue their own wishes. They may regress to earlier stages of functioning; withdraw from mastering their world, not impose their own assertiveness on others; accept a passive position; or, under other pathological circumstances, turn their aggression against themselves. They may become accident prone or develop psychosomatic disorders. Such children may deny their own interests and seem primarily superego-oriented rather than ego-oriented (see chapter 7, "Superego Development"). As a reaction formation to mask aggression, they may show excessive generosity and excessive concern for others.

Aggression may be expressed as passive resistance, dawdling, "accidentally" hurting others, or "accidentally" being destructive with toys or materials. At times, the only way some children can express their aggression may be by fantasies.

Conflict is suggested if there is insufficient aggression and inhibition of assertive-aggressive strivings. This may lead to constriction of initiative and denial of his own pleasure or restriction or any demonstration of affection.

On the other hand, some children may be too aggressive, so that it interferes with interpersonal relationships. Marked aggression, such as cruelty, sadistic behavior, or deliberately destructive behaviors, raises questions about the child's developmental progression.

2. See Ruediger Schroeer and Dorothy Flapan, "Assessing Aggressive and Friendly Behaviors in Young Children," *Journal of Psychology* 77: 193-202, 1971; and Ruediger Schroeer and Dorothy Flapan, "Aggressive and Friendly Behaviors of Young Children from Two Social Classes," *Child Psychiatry and Human Development* 2: 32-41, 1971.

The child's aggressive strivings are, as has been discussed earlier, continuously in interplay with the libidinal pleasure-seeking strivings—the reality and the social context within which a child lives. The process is complex, and the expression of the aggressive strivings is intertwined with other aspects of the child's life. When a child is extremely destructive, it is clear that we are witnessing abnormal aggressive strivings. It is more difficult to understand a child when his aggression is primarily expressed in fantasies. However, we may see in play his destructive interest and can then be alerted to his pathological aggression.

It is important to note that the aggressive strivings are often linked to sibling rivalry. Until now, we have spoken of rivalry only in connection with the oedipal constellation, but children who have older or younger siblings may play out that rivalry with other children. Aggressive feelings toward a sibling may become mixed with dependency or with affection, and then an older sibling may be admired and resented at the same time; or, there may be a wish to eliminate a younger sibling. The rivalry stimulates the assertive-competitive aims of the child and may then also appear in the nursery school or other group situations with peers.

In addition, it can be observed that a child may sometimes identify with a person who is very aggressive. This identification with the aggressor—even if the aggressor is against the child—is another modality of alliance and incorporation of aggression which may lead to various pathological features.

The preceding are only a few examples that demonstrate the many ways in which aggression is mixed with other interests and how it influences behavior.

In the longitudinal research study, it had been found that the content of the child's play, his fantasies, his overt expression of aggression and affection, as well as his lack of assertive-aggressive behavior and affectionate behavior, and his responses to the aggression and affection of others, could be observed and reported by adults who were in regular contact with the children—even though these items are not customarily emphasized in reports about the children. The specific items selected from the more extensive outline and included in the Short Assessment Outline give a valid and reliable indication of the current developmental status of the child's aggressive drive.[3]

3. See Appendix B for discussion of validity and reliability.

Criteria for Assessing
PHASE DEVELOPMENT

Phase	Characteristic, expected, typical	Uncharacteristic, unexpected, atypical, pathological	
		Pleasure-seeking	
		Ranging from:	To:
Infant: birth to 1½ (Oral Phase)	Able to find satiation-pleasure in eating, sucking, oral exploring or mouthing, biting, chewing, kissing. Able to give self gratification, e.g., thumb- or finger-sucking, sucking pacifier, toys. Pleasure from the natural rhythm of sleeping-resting. Pleasure in body functions. Pleasure in exploration. Pleasure in use of musculature — movements of body, arms, legs; turning, sitting, crawling.	Great indulgence in oral behaviors — voracious, overeating; continues frequent bottles beyond usual age of weaning; extensive oral exploring. Frequent and prolonged thumb- or finger-sucking, sucking other objects, mouthing. Frequent demands for body contact, being held. Extended periods of sleeping — "too much" sleeping, as if to avoid the world, escape. Much biting, grinding teeth, spitting, drooling.	No pleasure from eating — poor appetite, finicky eater, eats very little, habitually vomits. "Rejects" food. No attempts to give self gratification when it is lacking in the situation — does not show the expected oral exploring or mouthing, sucking, etc. No pleasure from body contact; avoids body contact; pushes away when held or cuddled. Resists going to sleep; restlessness in sleep; bad dreams; wakefulness. "Fights" sleep.
Toddler: 1½ to 3 (Anal Phase)	Pleasure in acquiring control of own body functions — urinating, defecating. Pleasure in use of musculature, large and small, and in acquiring control — climbing, walking, handling objects. Body control in relation to time and place. Pleasure in movement.	Toileting (and/or eating and/or sleeping) used as a statement vs. object ("I won't *because* you want me to") or as source of contention. Anal zone unduly eroticized. Asking to be wiped after toileting; not wiping self well. Diarrhea (no control). Aggressive use of wetting or soiling (because disappointed in mother or suffering object loss). Excessive use of musculature — hyperactive, reckless. Frequent soiling, bed-wetting, day-wetting.	No pleasure from body functions. Denies pleasure for self. Holding in — constipation. Excessive control. Disgust with body functions as reaction formation. Extremely clean and fussy with regard to body functions. Restricted use of musculature. Restricted in activity, cautious. Overly compulsive re toileting and/or cleanliness. Overly shy about excretory functions and procedures.

Differentiating Stage: 3 to 4½ (Phallic Phase)	Able to find pleasure in masturbation, playing with genitals, handling other parts of own body, e.g., playing with hair, stroking arm. Enjoyment of being nude, exhibiting self, "showing off." Pleasure in "poking," "piercing." Enjoyment of dressing up, looking handsome /pretty.	Frequent and prolonged masturbation — as reassurance and/or for comfort; intensive handling of own body or hair — "I can't stop." Excessive exhibiting of self — to get attention or as reassurance against own doubts. Buffoonery or clowning as distortion of exhibitionism — "showing off" displaced from asset to defect. Excessive attempts to get attention. Constantly wanting to dress up, "look handsome/pretty," as reassurance against own doubts.	Denies self pleasure, masturbation; avoids exploring own body. Inhibition of masturbation. Inhibition of nudity. Excessive modesty — as reaction formation of exhibitionistic tendencies. Shame re body. Reaction against exhibitionism appears as neglect of dress and/or hair. Avoids attention. May be "bored" as a result of suppressing masturbation or fantasies re masturbation.
Family Integration: 4½ to 6 (Oedipal Phase)	Pleasure in exploring; in achievement; in mastering difficulties; in solving problems; in coping with novel situations. For *boys*: pleasure in "masculine" activities; in being "a little man," in identifying with father, in flirting with women and girls. For *girls*: pleasure in "feminine" activities; in being "a little woman," a "little mother," in identifying with mother, in flirting with men and boys.	"Pushes" self to achieve — to overcome own doubts. "Pushes" self to master difficult situations. "Pushes" self to explore; to solve problems. For *boys*: "pushes" self to engage in masculine activities; to prove masculinity; "pushes" self to be "a little man." Avoids *all* feminine activities. Exaggerated interest in masculinity. Excessive flirting with females. For *girls*: "pushes" self to engage in feminine activites to prove femininity; "pushes" self to be "a little mother." Avoids *all* masculine activities. Exaggerated interest in femininity. Excessive flirting with males.	Inhibits exploring, achieving, succeeding in difficult situations. Minimal pleasure in achievement, in exploring. For *boys*: avoids masculine activities; engages in feminine activities. Inhibits flirtatiousness with females. For *girls*: avoids feminine activities; engages in masculine activities. Inhibits flirtatiousness with males.

Criteria for Assessing
PHASE DEVELOPMENT

Themes and/or Central Issues

Phase	Characteristic, expected, typical	Uncharacteristic, unexpected, atypical, pathological	
		Ranging from:	To:
Infant: birth to 1½ (Oral Phase)	Concern about object being there — losing the caretaking person, being abandoned, being left alone (fear of annihilation due to loss of caretaking object). Concern about being given care — being neglected. Concern about being satisfied — being deprived; getting his share — not getting his share; devouring — being devoured.	Intense concern about losing the caretaking person, being abandoned — "I *can't* be without you" — panic when caretaking person out of sight. Intense concern about being given care — continually needing and demanding care; being greedy; seeing others as unfair. Intense concern about being satisfied — deprived; getting his share; "taking in." Intense anxiety about being devoured.	No bond established with the caretaking person; little interest in presence or absence of the object. Little expectation of being given care; child has "given up," is apathetic, uninvolved. Indifferent to satisfaction; may even "reject" satisfaction. Swings between extremes of demanding satisfaction and care, and exaggerated indifference.
Toddler: 1½ to 3 (Anal Phase)	Concern whether can control others or will be controlled by others (omnipotence-helplessness). Concern about giving in to others. Concern whether will lose love of objects (if say no); concern about pleasing authority (fear of criticism and punishment). Concern whether can establish own control system, can control self or will "lose control." Includes concern about cleanliness-dirtiness, orderliness-disarray, keeping-losing, aggression (hurting —	Intense concern about being controlled by others; *has* to control them to avoid being controlled. Intense concern about losing love of object — continually seeking reassurance, trying to please, behaving so as not to incur any criticism. Extreme concern about losing control of self — becomes overcontrolled, rather than admit does not want to control self. Great concern about cleanliness-dirtiness, orderliness-disorderliness, keeping (hoarding), aggression by self	Fearful of controlling others; tries to get others to control him. Fearful of showing concern about losing love of object. Goes to opposite extreme — acts as if does not want love, is unconcerned about pleasing. Fights against controlling self — appears to lack control of self; will *not* control self. Swings between extremes of overcontrol and lack of control.

Phase	Characteristic, expected, typical	Uncharacteristic, unexpected, atypical, pathological	
		Ranging from:	To:
	getting hurt, destroying — being destroyed).	or others (hurting others or getting hurt).	
Differentiating Stage: 3 to 4½ (Phallic Phase)	Concern about being extraordinary (special) or worthless, being admired-ridiculed; concern about size (being bigger-smaller), about strength (being powerful — strong or weak — vulnerable); concern about being attractive-unattractive. For *boys*: concern about male attributes, intactness and damage to body, castration, appearance as a boy; concern about *being* a boy, own worth as a boy. For *girls*: concern about female attributes; appearance as a girl; concern about *being* a girl, own worth as a girl.	As reaction to feeling worthless, great emphasis on being special, being admired (with fear of being ridiculed). As reaction to feeling small and weak, great emphasis on being big and strong and powerful. Great preoccupation with being attractive, admired, lovable. As reaction to concern about body-damage, castration, takes risks unnecessarily. For *boys*: intense concern about masculinity and efforts constantly to show masculinity; anxiety about being castrated and constant anticipation of being castrated and protective maneuvers to prevent castration. For *girls*: intense concern about femininity and efforts constantly to show femininity. Or, resigns self to "second-class" status and accentuates worthlessness as a girl.	Denial of special worth — may appear as overly modest; may act in ways to prove worthlessness. Fear of being big and strong, so emphasizes smallness and weakness and vulnerability. Lack of interest in appearance; or going to the opposite extreme and denying any interest in appearance. Denies desire to be lovable — acts unlovable. For *boys*: denial of interest in own maleness; appears unmasculine. For *girls*: denial of interest in being feminine; appears unfeminine. Denial of "second-class" status as a girl and efforts to show she is more worthy than a boy; constantly competing with boys.

Phase	Characteristic, expected, typical	Uncharacteristic, unexpected, atypical, pathological	
		Ranging from:	To:
Family Integration: 4½ to 6 (Oedipal Phase)	For *boys*: concern about being like or different from father; about competing with mother for father; about competing with mother for father; concern about succeeding in competing with father as a male, persevering, or giving up because dare not succeed; concern about replacing father; concern about loving-getting rid of father. For *girls*: concern about being like or different from mother; about competing with mother for father and competing with father for mother; concern about succeeding in competing with mother as a female, persevering, or giving up because dare not succeed; concern about replacing mother; concern about loving-getting rid of mother. For both boys and girls: concern about sex, reproduction, marriage.	For *boys*: doubts he is like father, intense concern to prove he is like father; intense competition with father; great concern that mother prefers him to father; intense concern about being better than father. For *girls*: doubts she is like mother, intense concern to prove she is like mother; intense competition with mother; great concern that father prefers her to mother; intense concern about being better than mother. For *both*: overly concerned about sex, reproduction, marriage.	For *boys*: fear of being like father; tries to be different from father; fear of consequences if competes with father and succeds; strong need to fail. Avoids mother because of the danger, or avoids father. Appears to have great fear of females and/or males. Cannot let self replace father. For *girls*: fear of being like mother; tries to be different from mother; fear of consequences if competes with mother and succeeds; strong need to fail. Avoids father because of the danger, or avoids mother. Appears to have great fear of males and/or females. Cannot let self replace mother. For *both*: absence of any interest in sex, reproduction, marriage.

Criteria for Assessing
PHASE DEVELOPMENT

Play and Interests

Phase	Characteristic, expected, typical	Uncharacteristic, unexpected, atypical, pathological	
		Ranging from:	To:
Infant: birth to 1½ (Oral Phase)	Play at feeding and being fed; being "baby," being taken care of; eating, swallowing, devouring and being eaten, swallowed, devoured; biting others and being bitten. Play at losing and finding (as in peek-a-boo games, or hiding and finding toys, or dropping things and having them returned). Play at sleeping.	Intensive interest and/or prolonged play re feeding and being fed; being "baby"; devouring and/or being devoured. Intensive interest and/or prolonged play re losing and finding — people, things, toys.	Avoidance of playing "baby"; playing at devouring or being devoured. "Panic" or other strong reaction in refusing such play. Little interest in surroundings — in touching, handling.
Toddler: 1½ to 3 (Anal Phase)	Sublimation of anal and urethral preoccupation in painting, finger painting, modeling clay, water play, play with sand, other "messing" activities or dirtying activities. "Toilet" play. Play at being angry, scolding, at "destroying"; at hurting and getting punished or being hurt (e.g., with dolls). Play at being witch, devil, monster. Collecting materials and toys; some hoarding. Interest in bowel movements; in toileting — his own and others; in buttocks — his own and others.	Intensive interest and/or prolonged play with water, sand, clay, paint, "messing," "dirtying." Extreme messiness, dirtyness. Great amount of "toilet" talk, "toilet" play. Much angry play; much destructive play; much hurting play. Destructive with materials and toys. Much teasing play, scaring other children. Extreme wastefulness. Intensive interest and/or prolonged attention to body functions; much concern expressed and much discussion of them.	Avoidance of painting, finger painting, modeling clay, water play, play with sand, "messing" activities or "dirtying" activities. Extreme cleanliness and orderliness. Denial of body functions and avoidance of any "toilet" talk or "toilet" play. Cannot let self engage in any angry play or any destructive play. Inhibits expression of anger even in play. "Saves" materials, is cautious, thrifty, in their use; much hoarding.

Phase	Characteristic, expected, typical	Uncharacteristic, unexpected, atypical, pathological	
		Ranging from:	To:
Differentiating Stage: 3 to 4½ (Phallic Phase)	Interest in looking at others' genitals, touching; showing own genitals to others; watching others dressing, bathing, nude. Questions about differences between boys and girls. As sublimation of sexual curiosity, enjoys taking things apart to see what is inside, what makes them work. Investigative play. For *boys*: engages in boy-type play — play at shooting, stabbing, warring; play with cars and trucks and airplanes; play at social roles, such as policeman, fireman, milkman, and other culturally emphasized roles; play with both sexes. For *girls*: engages in girl-type play — play at mothering and homemaking; play with dolls; play at social roles of ballerina, nurse, teacher, and other culturally emphasized roles; play with both sexes.	Great interest in and/or prolonged attention to looking at others' genitals, showing own; watching others dressing, bathing, nude. Continuous and /or prolonged questioning about differences between boys and girls. Constantly taking things apart; investigative play. For *boys*: great emphasis on boy-type play and avoidance of *all* activities considered characteristic of girls. For *girls*: great emphasis on girl-type play and avoidance of *any* boy-type play; avoidance of *all* activities considered characteristic of boys.	Denial of *any* interest in genitals. Avoidance of looking at others and/or showing self. Extreme modesty. Denial of *any* sexual curiosity. Avoidance of questions about differences between boys and girls. Embarrassed by such discussions or references. For *boys*: avoidance of boy-type play; great interest in girl-type play and activities considered characteristic of girls. For *girls*: avoidance of girl-type play; great interest in boy-type play and activities considered characteristic of boys. Little play at social roles — male or female.

| Phase | Characteristic, expected, typical | Uncharacteristic, unexpected, atypical, pathological | |
		Ranging from:	To:
Family Integration: 4½ to 6 (Oedipal Phase)	Much time in family play — playing same-sex parent, most of the time; but sometimes playing child or opposite-sex parent. Some sex play. Talk about wanting to marry, about wanting to be a parent (father/mother). Girls play at being hostess, developing social skills; boys play at being guest. Questions about where babies come from; interest in taking care of a baby. Interest in exploring, learning. Interest in social activities of the group. Complex dramatic play. Interest in small-group games. Play at achieving, mastering difficulties, solving problems.	Practically all the time is spent in family play, to the exclusion of other kinds of play. Much sex play. Constant talk about wanting to marry. Excessive questioning about where babies come from. Intense interest in exploring, learning. Intense interest in the group. Forces self to enter and deal with difficult situations — in an effort to overcome own anxieties and doubts. For *boys*: great emphasis on *always* playing daddy; unwilling to take other roles in play. Constant talk about wanting to be a father. For *girls*: great emphasis on *always* playing mother; unwilling to take other roles in play. Constant talk about wanting to be a mother.	Avoidance of any family play. Avoidance of *any* sex play. Avoidance of any talk about marrying or about being a parent (father or mother). Uncomfortable in such discussions. Acts naive. Avoidance of any questions about where babies come from. Embarrassed by such talk. Denies interest in exploring, learning and/or avoids exploring-learning activities. Denies interest in social activities of the group and/or avoids group. Insists on setting up own individual play — extreme degree of independence and isolation.

Criteria for Assessing PHASE DEVELOPMENT

Character Traits

Phase	Characteristic, expected, typical	Uncharacteristic, unexpected, atypical, pathological	
		Ranging from:	To:
Infant: birth to 1½ (Oral Phase)	Passive — expects to be given to. Receptive — to what is given. Dependent — for physical and emotional needs; some attempts to be independent. Wanting to be "fed" — demanding. Compliant — as a way to get needs met. Trusting — in expectation needs will be met and he will be taken care of.	Fearful (anxious?) and therefore clinging for gratification and protection. Extremely passive and/or dependent. Extremely compliant, obedient, submissive, ingratiating — so as to be taken care of. Much whining.	Complains about not getting enough; wants what others have; sees others treating him unfairly. Always wants more, greedy, grabbing, extremely demanding, insistent. Because disappointed in object or frustrated, has turned away and become precociously independent. *Cannot* be dependent, receptive, fed. Untrusting. Swings between being extremely independent and extremely demanding.
Toddler: 1½ to 3 (Anal Phase)	Emphasis on "me" and "mine." Attempts to control others. Some bossiness, some dominating. Efforts to protect self from being controlled by others. Negative, defiant, opposing, stubborn, obstinate. Teasing; quarrelsomeness. Ambivalent; indecisive. Efforts to be clean, orderly, punctual; to control self.	Extreme resistance to control by others. Extreme negativism, defiance, opposition, stubborness, obstinacy, quarrelsomeness. Much bossiness; very dominating; very controlling of others. Much teasing; much insulting others. Easily feels insulted, hurt. Sadistic — seems to enjoy hurting others. Extreme ambivalence: extreme indecisiveness; clinging as expression of ambivalence and/or control rather than for protection. Will not be orderly, punctual, clean. Absence of self-control.	Unaggressiveness as indication of conflict with anal striving. Child presents too little trouble and difficulty for adults; will *not* permit self to be negative, defiant, stubborn, quarrelsome. *Must* agree. Masochistic — seems to enjoy being hurt. As reaction against wish to be bossy, dominate, control others — lets self be bossed, dominated, controlled. Extremely orderly, punctual, clean. Overly self-controlled.

Phase	Characteristic, expected, typical	Uncharacteristic, unexpected, atypical, pathological	
		Ranging from:	To:
Differentiating Stage: 3 to 4 (Phallic Phase)	Competing (to be best, biggest, strongest, most attractive, most loved); challenging others; bragging-boasting. Exhibitionistic — admiring self, proud of self. Seeking attention. Forceful, assertive, "thrusting" (girls not as forceful as boys).	Extremely competitive ; continually challenging others, bragging. Exhibiting self, "showing self off"; constantly seeking attention of adults and/or other children by questioning, talking, performing, clowning, provoking. Preoccupation with being attractive, admired, lovable. *Boys* show exaggerated "masculinity" as overcompensation for own fears and doubts (e.g., castration fear). *Girls* show exaggerated "femininity."	Does not dare to assert self — appears passive. Avoids competing, challenging. As reaction against wish to exhibit, is extremely retiring, shy. Avoids *any* exhibitionism. Avoids attention Becomes embarrassed when given attention. Denies desire to be lovable — acts in unlovable ways to prove it. *Boys* deny "masculinity" — cannot be active, aggressive, tough. *Girls* deny "femininity" — cannot meet cultural expectations, cannot let self be gentle; act more like a boy than a girl — tough, aggressive.

Phase	Characteristic, expected, typical	Uncharacteristic, unexpected, atypical, pathological	
		Ranging from:	To:
Family Integration: 4½ to 6 (Oedipal Phase)	Seductive, manipulating, "appealing." Responsive, friendly, cooperative. Charming with opposite sex (adults and children), flirtatious, coy. Competing with same sex (adults and children) and then often appeasing. Challenging same sex — establishing own sexual identity.	Extremely manipulative. Exaggerated seductiveness. Extremely flirtatious with the opposite sex (adults and children). Unable to cooperate. Distant. Constantly competing with same sex.	Self-defeating in encounters with same sex (adults and children). Self-punishing. Avoids opposite sex — may rebuff them. Unable to compete with same sex. Overly cooperative, "too nice," too friendly, too responsive. Constantly appeasing same sex.

Criteria for Assessing
PHASE DEVELOPMENT

Problems and/or Symptoms

Phase	Characteristic, expected, typical	Uncharacteristic, unexpected, atypical, pathological	
		Ranging from:	To:
Infant: birth to 1½ (Oral Phase)	Oral autoerotic gratification — sucking thumb, finger, toys, etc; drooling, spitting, licking lips; sticking out tongue, rolling tongue. Occasional eating problems. Occasional sleep disturbances. Rocking, swaying, other rhythmical movements.	Continual eating problems — refusing to eat, vomiting, fussy eater, etc. Much biting self, others, toys, etc. Continual sleep disturbances, nightmares. Much rocking, head-banging. Much restless activity; "high." Frequent and prolonged crying. Excessive irritability.	Chronically engaging in oral auto-erotic behaviors such as sucking. Chronically depressed, dejected. Apathetic.
Toddler: 1½ to 3 (Anal Phase)	Needs some assistance after toileting, such as pulling up pants. Resists going to bed or resting. Needs special blanket or toy to sleep or rest. Some conflict over eating, dressing, etc. Compulsions, rituals, obsessions. Avoidance of or flight from anxiety-provoking situations. Magical thinking.	Frequent bed-wetting, pants-wetting. Diarrhea. Frequent soiling. Refuses to wipe self. Asks to be wiped after toileting. Chews things. Extreme and persistent anger. Much destructive behavior. Extremely dirty, disorderly, wasteful.	Refuses to toilet except at home. Chronic constipation. Picks at fingers, scabs, nose. Bites fingernails; grinds teeth. Cannot express aggression toward others — turns it inward. Extreme cleanliness, orderliness, hoarding.

Phase	Characteristic, expected, typical	Uncharacteristic, unexpected, atypical, pathological	
		Ranging from:	To:
Differentiating Stage: 3 to 4½ (Phallic Phase)	Phobias, fears. Realistic fears are age-appropriate. Fears as response to danger, to feelings of helplessness. Some fears about being hurt, about bodily damage. Some masturbation, handling or holding genitals, stroking skin, stroking or twisting hair.	Keeps fears hidden. Cannot admit fears or show fears. Maintains "brave front." Too few fears are observable. Denies fears. Severe nightmares or bad dreams. Frequent and prolonged masturbation. Excessive concern re being hurt, damaged.	Extensive and/or intensive phobias and fears, e.g., panic re cat or dog. Fears frequently interfere with functioning. Denial of any pleasure in own body. Inhibits any masturbation or auto-erotic activity.
Family Integration: 4½ to 6 (Oedipal Phase)	Temporary regression to symptoms or problems of earlier phases. Some guilt re own wishes and fantasies.	Prolonged regression to earlier phases, e.g., soiling, wetting, excessive oral behaviors and activities.	Great fear of males and/or females. Great fear of leaving parent — as reaction against own destructive wishes. Excessive guilt. Fear of growing up to be a "bad" man or a "bad" woman.

Criteria for Assessing
PHASE DEVELOPMENT

Assertion–Aggression

Phase	Characteristic, expected, typical	Uncharacteristic, unexpected, atypical, pathological	
		Ranging from:	To:
Infant: birth to 1½ (Oral Phase)	Expresses wants, makes demands, imposes self on world. No consideration for others. Grabs. Reacts to restraint with aggression; with crying, yelling, striking out. Also, reacts to interruption of activity and to delay of gratification. Can be diverted, placated. Oral aggression — "biting," "devouring."	Continually expressing wants, making demands. Maximally imposes self on environments; little effort to adjust to environment. Frequent displays of strong aggression — global, undifferentiated rage — for extended periods of time. Cannot be diverted, placated. Much oral aggression — biting, oral attacking, devouring.	Minimally imposes self on environment; usually tries to "adjust" self to demands of environment. Always tries to please, obey, comply. Extreme passivity. Undemanding. Helpless. Waits for others to give him what he desires or wishes. Seldom any display of aggression — even when it would be expected.
Toddler: 1½ to 3 (Anal Phase)	Anal aggressive. Swings between love and hate — ambivalence — libido and aggression not fused with each other. Enough aggression to go after what he wants and to reach goals. At times, aggressively controlling. Can usually control his own aggression — keep it within limits — though sometimes loses control. Tries to control others to some extent.	Extreme aggressivity. Aggression interferes with relations. Balance of love and hate swings toward hate, hostility, cruelty. Sadistic — much "hurting" others — insulting, teasing. Much hitting, kicking, scratching, throwing. Hurting by explosions of messy, destructive behavior. Outbursts of destruction. Uncontrolled aggression much of the time — destroys social relations. Great aggressiveness as reaction to fear.	Unaggressive. Cannot assert self. Reaction formation against sadistic impulses — overconcern re others' pains and wounds. Turns aggression on self. Accident-prone. Masochistic — much being hurt; easily feels insulted; sensitive to criticism. Hurting by keeping in, hiding feelings. Overcontrol of aggression. "Pacifism" as reaction to wish to attack or as expression of fear of being attacked. Little initiative; not enough aggression to reach goals; waits for help.

Phase	Characteristic, expected, typical	Uncharacteristic, unexpected, atypical, pathological	
		Ranging from:	To:
Differentiating Stage: 3 to 4½ (Phallic Phase)	Phallic aggressive. In most situations, able to express aggression in moderate amounts and in socially acceptable ways (in words and/or in actions). Some consideration for others. Independent achievement strivings. Can compete with other children for toys, favors, attention. Can show anger when appropriate; can assert self; can pursue own ends and get wants satisfied. Aggression channeled into acceptable expressions — poking, tickling, verbal provocations, exaggeration. Girls more often than boys may express aggression indirectly, and/or in fantasy.	Competitiveness may be extremely aggressive. Aggression as over-compensation for castration fear. Asserts self in extreme ways and/or attacks others. Fiercely pursues own ends. Marked aggression, externally directed, disrupts relations. Marked aggression is less typical of girls than of boys — but may come out by competing with boys, "castrating" boys.	Unable to show aggression directly, unable to assert self and/or unable to get what he wants. Inhibits aggression or expresses it in devious ways or in self-inflicted injuries. Psychosomatic disorders. Passive resistance, "accidentally" hurting others. Aggression expressed in fantasy rather than in activity. Girls are more likely to inhibit aggression than are boys.
Family Integration: 4½ to 6 (Oedipal Phase)	Balance between attempts to master (cope with) environment and attempts to satisfy own desire for pleasure (neutralization and fusion). Both the expressions of pleasure and of aggression checked by reality. Pleasure principle giving way to reality principle.	Extreme emphasis on attempts to master environment. Manipulates aggressively. May manipulate by being seductive. Particularly aggressive toward same-sex parent.	Little or no effort to master environment, manipulate others. Constriction of initiative. More "superego"-oriented than ego-oriented or reality-oriented. Excessive generosity as reaction formation to mask aggression.

Phase	Characteristic, expected, typical	Uncharacteristic, unexpected, atypical, pathological	
		Ranging from:	To:
	Ego-oriented, reality-oriented. Able to maintain satisfying relations with others and still get what he wants. Aggression may come out in show of initiative, in developing autonomy; in attempts to master environment or to take "social action."		

Response to Aggression by Others

Phase	Characteristic, expected, typical	Uncharacteristic, unexpected, atypical, pathological	
		Ranging from:	To:
Infant: birth to 1½ (Oral Phase)	Reacts to aggression by others with crying, yelling, striking back.	Prolonged and intense reaction to aggression by others.	Passively accepts others' aggression. Does not defend self or respond with counteraggression. Usually turns to adult for help; or, may just whine helplessly.
Toddler: 1½ to 3 (Anal Phase)	Reacts to others' aggression, but shows some control of his response. May use language, may shove other, may cry. Reaction is immediate and short-lived. May scold or criticize or lecture other.	Reacts in extremely aggressive and angry way to any display of aggression by others. May bite, kick, scratch, inflict injuries, throw blocks or toys. Overreacts, cannot control self. May scream, yell, strike out physically.	Weak response to aggression. Made anxious or fearful by display of even moderate aggression. May run away in fear, show hurt withdrawal, cry, or stand immobilized.
Differentiating Stage: 3 to 4½ (Phallic Phase)	Easily tolerates moderate show of aggression by others. Takes it in stride. May respond by asserting self, by acting aggressive in words or actions but in socially acceptable ways. Girls are more likely than boys to respond in verbal ways.	Cannot tolerate any show of aggression by others; overreacts. May become either extremely physically aggressive or extremely verbally aggressive. Violent attack, challenge.	Shows "superiority" by ignoring the aggression in obvious ways. May regress to passive, helpless acceptance of aggression.
Family Integration: 4½ to 6 (Oedipal Phase)	Response to aggression by others is increasingly verbal. Insistence on compromise, justice, democratic process. Girls more likely than boys to be peacemakers.	Regresses to earlier ways of responding to aggression by others.	Extreme guilt and blames self for being cause of others' aggression. Excessively appeasing to aggressive one.

Criteria for Assessing
PHASE DEVELOPMENT

Expression of Affection

Phase	Characteristic, expected, typical	Uncharacteristic, unexpected, atypical, pathological	
		Ranging from:	To:
Infant: birth to 1½ (Oral Phase)	Able to express affection — by hugging, cuddling, kissing, stroking — to mother and maybe other family members.	Excessive show of affection; overly affectionate (continually hugging, kissing, touching, stroking others). Affection as a way of clinging for protection and gratification, for reassurance.	Shows only limited expression of affection, if any — only to mother or mother-substitute.
Toddler: 1½ to 3 (Anal Phase)	Able to express affection in actions, and sometimes verbally, to family members and an occasional friend of the family who is familiar.	Uses affection as a way of controlling others, as a way of being aggressive — e.g., hugging too hard. Excessive affection.	Inhibits or restricts demonstrations of affection. Very selective re persons toward whom shows affection. Uninterested in showing any affection. It is not that he inhibits affection he feels, but rather he does not *experience* affectionate feelings.
Differentiating Stage: 3 to 4½ (Phallic Phase)	Able to express affection verbally and in actions — to family members, teachers, and/or peers — in an easy and unselfconscious way.	Intense show of affection. Indiscriminate re object of affection. May use affection in exhibitionistic way. Overly affectionate.	Uneasy about expressing any affection. Limited expression of affection. Show of affection may be accompanied by embarrassment, self-consciousness, silliness, clowning. May express affection only in indirect, devious ways. May express affection primarily in fantasy.

Phase	Characteristic, expected, typical	Uncharacteristic, unexpected, atypical, pathological	
		Ranging from:	To:
Family Integration: 4½ to 6 (Oedipal Phase)	Especially affectionate with parent of opposite sex and with other substitutes for this parent. Less affectionate with same-sex parent and with other substitutes for this parent.	Uses affection in extremely manipulative ways. Overly affectionate with opposite-sex parent and with substitutes for this parent. Unable to show any affection for same-sex parent or with substitutes for this parent.	Unable to be affectionate — especially with opposite-sex parent and with substitutes for this parent.

Criteria for Assessing
PHASE DEVELOPMENT

Response to Affection by Others

Phase	Characteristic, expected, typical	Uncharacteristic, unexpected, atypical, pathological	
		Ranging from:	To:
Infant: birth to 1½ (Oral Phase)	Able to accept affection from mother and other family members. Responds to affectionate overtures. Enjoys being cuddled, kissed, hugged, stroked.	Overly responsive to affection — undiscriminating about who is giving it — "hungry" for it.	Unresponsive to affection — "as if numb." Cannot let himself be cuddled. Pushes out of person's arms or lap. Does not like to be kissed, hugged, handled.
Toddler: 1½ to 3 (Anal Phase)	Accepts affection in an easy way from family and familiar adults or children, and may even appear pleased by it. At times may refuse, as a way of showing he is in control of the situation. Negativistic.	Usually searching for affection; shows anxiety about the possible loss of affection. Asks for demonstrations of affection and for reassurance. If affection is shown, may respond by becoming overaffectionate. Seeks affection to counteract own ambivalence and negativism.	Uncomfortable about accepting affection from others and untrusting of their affection. Sees affection as attempt to control him. May reject or withdraw from all affectionate overtures from others. May be able to accept only limited expressions of affection from certain persons. Uninterested in and unresponsive to any affection from others. Does not look for affection or expect it.
Differentiating Stage: 3 to 4½ (Phallic Phase)	Responds to affection by peers, as well as by teacher and other familiar adults.	Affection accepted with embarrassment, self-consciousness, silliness, clowning, hyperactivity.	Shy in response to affection. May show uneasiness when others are affectionate.
Family Integration: 4½ to 6 (Oedipal Phase)	More responsive to affection from opposite-sex parent, or substitutes for that parent, than to affection from same-sex parent.	Overly responsive to affection from opposite-sex parent. Rejects any affection from same-sex parent.	Rejects affection from opposite-sex parent. Overly responsive to affection from same-sex parent.

Chapter 7
Superego Development

The moral development of a child—or the development of the *superego*—is another aspect which is important to assess. The superego is the expression of the emerging values of the child, his capacity to differentiate between right and wrong, his anticipation of and reaction to punishment, and his guilt. *Superego* refers to the child's internalization of parental prohibitions and values, his adjustments to the social standards of his cultural group, his ego ideal, and the consequent positive or negative feelings about himself or attitudes toward himself.

Stages of Superego Development

Infant: Birth to One-and-a-Half Years (Oral Phase)

This aspect of development differs from other aspects in that there is no evidence of superego development in the infant. The superego, which becomes an internalized, independent part of psychic organization, comes to the fore later, although there is early evidence of forerunners of what in time will become superego. Superego is a psychic organization which has to achieve its own structure and is relatively independent from external supporting influences over a period of years.

In the oral phase of development, the infant does not "know" yet the difference between right and wrong, good and bad, which acts are approved of and which disapproved of, and what he *should* do and what he should *not* do. The infant acts to gratify impulses whether or not an adult is present. He does not, in the beginning, anticipate punishment or "feel guilty." Gradually, however, he learns to respond when someone says, "No." Should he be punished or reprimanded for his actions, he may cry, look hurt, withdraw, or move on to other activities. He does not as yet have a "self" to feel "good" or "bad" about, nor does he have an ego-ideal.

Toddler: One-and-a-Half to Three Years (Anal Phase)

During the anal phase of development, the toddler learns the general principle that some actions are considered "good" by the environment and some "bad," that some behaviors are regarded as "right" and some "wrong." He also learns which of his specific actions are approved and which disapproved by the members of his family. He comes to understand that certain behaviors will be rewarded by the members of his family and other behaviors punished, and he may avoid punishable behaviors when others are present, although he may engage in them in the absence of the adults. In this early period of development, the child relies primarily on the external reactions of others to determine right and wrong and to influence his actions. These early interactions lead to the precursors of the superego.

In time, the toddler acts in ways his parents consider "good" and avoids those actions his parents consider "bad." Occasionally, he may even ask them questions about what is the right way to act and what is the wrong way.

At times, he may take the role of the authority figure toward himself, scolding himself for what he has just done or slapping his own hand. Also, he may take the role of parent and "teach" his dolls, stuffed animals, or family pets which behaviors are approved and which disapproved within this environment.

With experience, the toddler begins to anticipate punishment for "wrongdoing" and to try in various ways to avoid it. He may blame others for what happened—someone else in the family, an imaginary friend, a doll, or a pet. He may deny that he acted as he did or that what happened really did happen, in spite of the obvious evidence. He may try to hide so as not to be discovered. If he is reprimanded or punished for his actions, he may seek reassurance afterwards that he is still loved and accepted, even though he had been punished.

We can begin to observe some expressions of developing guilt in the toddler. Even during the second year of life, if a child has done something which is against the standards and expectations of his parents, we can see from the child's hesitation or from the way he looks at the adults that he realizes that he has done something which will not be tolerated or which will lead to criticism. During this period of negativism, however, he may do it anyway, even though there will be unwanted consequences. What appears to be guilt at this phase of development is primarily related to the fear of punishment and to the fear that the adult may withdraw affection. Such expressions of fear are as yet not internalized, and there is not yet an independent, internal psychic structure. Instead, the fear is still strongly regulated by the interplay with the environment.

There are, however, some children who, during the second or third year of life, have already organized strong rules within themselves of what is permitted, what is tolerated, and what order of action should be achieved. They will express much concern about cleanliness and washing their hands; they will not tolerate the arrangement of play materials or tools to be different from what they "should" be. They thus show the influence of an ego and superego organization which is already beginning to express rigidity and insufficient flexibility.

With regard to self-esteem, the toddler feels "good" when he is praised or rewarded by the adults for his behavior and feels "bad" when he is criticized, punished, or reprimanded. His evolving self and his self-feelings depend on the evaluations of others and their esteem for him.

Differentiating Stage: Three to Four-and-a-Half Years (Phallic Phase)

By the phallic phase of development, the child "knows" the dif-- ference between right and wrong, as defined by his family members and their social group. He "knows" which behaviors are approved and which are disapproved, which rewarded and which punished by the adults in his environment. And he is learning which behaviors are considered "appropriate" for a boy and which for a girl in his social group.

The child, by this stage, may be "good" and "act right" even though an adult is not present. He shows some awareness or concern about the "goodness" and "badness" of others. He may criticize "bad" children to the adults, or he may warn other children not to be "bad."

His own actions and those of others are judged as "good" or "bad' in terms of the responses of the adults. Thus, actions which have the most serious consequences (that is, which are most strongly reprimanded, criticized, or punished) are judged most severely, in contrast to older children who will take into account the motivations of the actor in addition to the consequences.

The phallic child is learning to respect others' possessions and rights. He can accept limits and the authority of the adults in his environment. He will try to follow directions and rules. The phallic child expects to be punished should he exceed the set limits or "break the rules." He may try, however, to lessen the punishment by promising *never* to act that way again or by explaining, "It was an accident."

When he is reprimanded or punished, he shows feelings of being injured or ashamed. He has negative feelings about himself when he is "bad" or acts inappropriately and positive feelings about himself when he is "good" or acts appropriately. Girls in this phase are usually more "socialized" than boys and are more strict with themselves than boys, especially at school and in other situations outside the home.

Feelings of pride and of shame can be observed. The phallic child is proud of being himself, as well as proud of what he can accomplish and of his socially appropriate behaviors. He feels attractive and worthwhile and usually has a high self-opinion.

Family Integration: Four-and-a-Half to Six Years (Oedipal Phase)

During the family integration phase of development, the child idealizes and identifies with his parents and wants to comply with their demands. He will, however, experience serious conflicts during this phase since his inner awareness of good and bad has come into the foreground of his new developmental capacities. This awareness will affect his pleasure-seeking as well as his aggressive strivings. In taking over the role of the parents, the child, through his superego, regulates his drives and inhibits drive expression through approval and disapproval. He is much better equipped to deal with the assessment of appropriate social behavior by the time he reaches this phase, but he is full of conflicts about it.

The oedipal child in his fantasies expresses his struggle with being good versus bad. This is now related to a triadic situation in which child, father, and mother are in interplay. They are part of the problem of finding a position in which he can do justice to his own wishes and ideals, and, at the same time, give due consideration to the positions of both parents.

The oedipal child restrains his wishes, feels guilty for them, and may anticipate punishment for even fantasizing about his wishes. He feels guilty even if no one knows about the fantasies.

For some children it is more difficult to develop standards, values, and ideals because they may observe inconsistencies between what the parents say *should* be done and what the parents themselves actually do. At times, there may also be confusion because the children encounter inconsistencies between what they have observed at home and what they are taught in school. During this period of internalizing, the same child may apply a standard in one area but not in another.

An ego-ideal has begun to develop. The *ego-ideal* represents what the individual child would like to be—his ambitions, goals, and ideals for himself. His self-esteem is affected by how he sees himself measuring up to his ideals. Observations can be made as to his efforts to maintain his self-esteem and actions or situations which interfere with his ego-ideal and lower his self-esteem. The child who achieves his own standards sees himself as successful, feels competent, and appears to others as a self-confident and secure person. He is usually proud of what he has done and takes pride in having done it well. His feelings of self-esteem are now related to his own standards and values, but judgments by others also influence his perception of himself and his self-esteem.

By this phase, the child has ideas about his responsibilities and about the extent to which he meets them. This also affects his feelings about himself. If he tries to live up to impossibly high standards, he will see himself as a failure or as "bad."

Indices of Development

By playing with the child, it is possible for an adult to obtain information regarding the child's ideas about "good" and "bad" or about what is the "right" or "wrong" thing to do in a given situation. It is possible also to obtain from observers descriptions of the ways the child responds to directions, limits, rules, and discipline. Furthermore, it can be determined whether the child needs the presence of an adult in order to live up to superego expectations or whether he is able to function with an equal degree of moral judgment when the adult authority is absent.

From such information, we can make inferences about the degree of internalization which has been achieved, and we may get clues about the extent to which an independent code of behavior is emerging. The observations can also provide us with indications of the child's ability to function outside the family environment—in school and in the community. We can see whether his behavior is appropriate to the social situation and to the rules and regulations which extra familial situations demand.

Moreover, by exploring the child's fantasies about his defiance of rules and regulations and his fantasies of anticipated punishment or disapproval, it is possible to make some inferences about the structure of his superego—whether it is consolidated, whether it is too severe and inhibits functioning by undue guilt and moral rigidity, or whether there are lacunae in the superego which permit a gratification of certain needs with insufficient consideration of social and moral issues.

It is possible to obtain some indications of the integration of the child's ego-ideal and self-esteem by observing the behaviors of which he is proud or ashamed, by learning his standards and his ideals for himself, as well as the extent to which he sees himself living up to them, and by determining his reactions to external evaluations such as praise and criticism.

The child's pride in himself, his assessment of his social standing in the group, and his estimate of the esteem others have for him are also indicators of his ego-ideal and superego function.

Symptoms

The superego may be too rigid, and therefore too restricting of behaviors, or too mild, and therefore insufficiently controlling of self-centered, inconsiderate wishes. When a child is overstrict with himself, overmoralistic with others, overly concerned about right and wrong and "badness," and too concentrated on being "good," we have indications of a superego disorder.

The child may express the strict superego demands by guilt, fears, or an oversensitive response to the approval or disapproval of the outside world. He might also show anxiety about seeing himself as a "bad" person, "hating" himself; or his guilt might be expressed in nightmares.

On the other hand, if a child, in response to his own wishes, acts in an antisocial way with insufficient consideration for others, we have an indication that the superego is not sufficiently developed. There are children who act to gratify infantile impulses (for example, taking others' belongings) or who act antisocially, whether or not an adult is present. They do not seem to know the difference between right and wrong. The superego has not developed as expected. Such children require extended reinforcement by the adults to learn about "right" and "wrong," since they continue to consider only their own wishes. These children may have been overindulged, "spoiled"; or they may not have had the opportunity to identify with a model who provides an example of moral, socially considered behavior.

There are some children who set their standards unrealistically high, so that they cannot meet them and therefore are doomed to see themselves as failures. Such children seem insecure about their abilities and usually do not feel proud of the work they do or of themselves. They show frequent shifts in self-esteem, influenced by the comments of others, especially authority figures. They are insecure about their social position, about being part of a group. They may express this insecurity in many different ways. One can observe frequent shifts from too great a friendliness to shyness and dependence on authority figures. The same insecurity may lead to isolation and to inability to join age-appropriate group functions.

Assessment of Superego Development

Adults are cognizant of the extent to which children respond or do not respond to rules and regulations and accept discipline in the home and in the school. They know which children still need to test limits and which are overly strict in following rules and regulations. It is interesting that adults often pay more attention to those children who violate rules than to those who follow rules and regulations too closely and rigidly.

It has not been customary for adults to refer to the child's ideals for himself or his attitudes toward himself. However, when the teachers and parents in our study were questioned about the ego-ideal or the self-esteem of a child, they were able to provide information. Recently these areas appear to have gained new interest; shyness and unsureness have been reported frequently, though these are not expressed in terms of the child's self-perception or self-esteem.

As with other aspects of development, the items included in the Short Assessment Outline were extracted from what had been included in the more comprehensive clinical study. Taken together, they resulted in an valid and reliable assessment of the child's superego development.[1]

1. See Appendix B for discussion of validity and reliability.

SUPEREGO DEVELOPMENT

Phase	Characteristic, expected, typical	Emegence of Superego	
		Uncharacteristic, unexpected, atypical, pathological	
		Ranging from:	To:
Infant: birth to 1½ (Oral Phase)	Does not yet "know" the difference between right and wrong, good and bad, which actions are approved and which disapproved, what he should do and what he should not do. Acts to gratify impulses, whether or not adult is present. May act "good" or "bad" depending on own impulses and desires. May act antisocially, take others' possessions, bite. Learning to respond when someone says "No." Learning inhibition of biting, grabbing.	Does not respond to "No." No inhibition of biting, grabbing, other antisocial actions.	Overresponds to "No" or to scolding or spanking. Withdraws into self. Becomes frightened and/or apathetic.
Toddler: 1½ to 3 (Anal Phase)	"Knows" in a gross way that some actions are considered good and some bad, some ways of behaving are regarded as right and some wrong. "Knows" which actions are approved and which disapproved by parents, what parents think he should do and should not do. Knows certain behaviors will be punished and avoids these when others are around. Says "No," but	Does not comply with parents' requests or demands. Little guilt. "Tests" limits of adult. May deliberately provoke adults, e.g., by breaking rules. Acts in ways he thinks are "good" only when an adult is present; little capacity to decide right and wrong — does not "know" specific actions approved or disapproved by par-	Perceives parents as very powerful, superhuman, supermoral. Always acts in ways he thinks "good," even when adult is not present. Can never let himself do anything "wrong" or "bad." Has to follow rules. Great concern about badness in self and others. Very strong feelings about right and wrong. Much questioning about what is good

Phase	Characteristic, expected, typical	Uncharacteristic, unexpected, atypical, pathological	
		Ranging from:	To:
	then follows directions. Most of the time acts in ways parents say are "good." May at times do things even though "knows" they are "bad." Can follow rules if adult present. May voice some concern about his badness and others'. May ask questions about what is right and wrong.	ents. Much variation, depending on whether at school or at home. No concern about disapproval or about badness.	and what is bad. Too afraid of disapproval.
Differentiating Stage: 3 to 4½ (Phallic Phase)	Knows difference between right and wrong, good and bad, as defined by his family members and their social group. Knows what behaviors are approved and disapproved by adults, rewarded and punished; also which behaviors are expected of boys and which of girls, which are considered appropriate for each sex. Criticizes others or complains about them not acting appropriately. Can accept limits; can accept authority. Respects others' possessions. Can share, can take turns most of the time. Can accept and follow rules and schedules, respond to sugges-	Usually does not accept rules or schedules, usually resistant to and does not follow directions. Does not comply with internal representatives of external demands. Will not share, will not take turns. Difficulty handling routines and/or transitions; will not accept authority. Difficulty accepting any "demands" made on him; resistant to any suggestions. Cannot accept limits, expressed in "acting-out."	Preoccupied with being good. Extremely conscientious. Expressed in fears or extreme orderliness. Strict with self and with others. Extremely polite. Rigid, desperate quality in following routines, following directions, accepting suggestions. Always follows rules, accepts authority. Great concern about following schedules. Must share — often gives the other a bigger share than self. Must take turns — often gives the other a longer turn than self. Makes rules for others, directs them.

Phase	Characteristic, expected, typical	Uncharacteristic, unexpected, atypical, pathological Ranging from:	To:
	routines and transitions, though at times may need help from adult. May be "good" even though adult is not present. (Girls more strict with self than are boys, especially at school and outside the home.) Awareness of and some concern about goodness-badness in others. Criticizes "bad" children and warns other children not to be "bad."		Preoccupied with being "correct," acting "right." Overly severe superego; great guilt. Regards most of his actions and thoughts as "bad," feels guilty, "hates" self. Even thinking something he thinks is "bad," child feels guilty, sees self as "bad," "hates" self.
Family Integration: 4½ to 6 (Oedipal Phase)	Beginning internalization of norms; autonomous "code" of behavior. Independent capacity to decide right and wrong in many instances. Forbids self to want certain things (e.g., opposite-sex parent) and feels guilty for wishes and anticipates punishment for them. Forbids self to do certain things and feels guilty after acts. More strict with self than at earlier age (girls more so than boys).	Little capacity to decide right and wrong. Little guilt. Little internalization of norms.	

Criteria for Assessing
SUPEREGO DEVELOPMENT

Phase	Characteristic, expected, typical	Punishment	
		Uncharacteristic, unexpected, atypical, pathological	
		Ranging from:	To:
Infant: birth to 1½ (Oral Phase)	Does not anticipate punishment. If punished or reprimanded, may cry, and then move on to other activities.	Punishment has little effect. May immediately return to the forbidden act.	Extreme reaction to punishment or reprimand — as if fears abandonment for being bad.
Toddler: 1½ to 3 (Anal Phase)	May take role of authority toward self — may scold self after doing something forbidden; may slap own hand. In play, may teach dolls or animals what is approved and disapproved. May anticipate punishment after wrong doing and try to avoid it by blaming others (such as another child, imaginary friend, pet). May deny the act actually happened. If reprimanded, may seek affection afterwards as reassurance.	Lack of concern about punishment, lack of interest in the rules.	Terrified of doing wrong, making a mistake. Extremely fearful of punishment. Sees faults in others and has punitive attitude toward them, as well as toward self. If reprimanded, acts as if he fears the loss of love. If reprimanded, must seek reassurance afterwards.
Differentiating Stage: 3 to 4½ (Phallic Phase)	After wrongdoing, expects punishment. Most of the time, takes it in stride. May try to lessen punishment by promising not to act that way again. If reprimanded, may act injured; may act ashamed.	Completely unconcerned about punishment and unaffected by it.	Extreme overreaction to punishment

Phase	Characteristic, expected, typical	Uncharacteristic, unexpected, atypical, pathological	
		Ranging from:	To:
Family Integration: 4½ to 6 (Oedipal Phase)	Expects punishment if breaks rules or acts in forbidden ways. When reprimanded, feels guilty. Feels guilty, even if no one else sees the wrongdoing, and may punish himself for what he has done or may try to make amends.	Shows no guilt. No anticipation of punishment for wrongdoing. No reaction to punishment; no regret, no indication of future change in actions.	Extremely guilty. *Always* anticipates punishment, even for minor acts. *Always* affected by punishment — extremely contrite: *having* to atone and make amends. Guilt may continue for extended time after punishment. May feel guilty even if he has not been punished.

Criteria for Assessing
SUPEREGO DEVELOPMENT

Self-Esteem

Phase	Characteristic, expected, typical	Uncharacteristic, unexpected, atypical, pathological	
		Ranging from:	To:
Infant: birth to 1½ (Oral Phase)	Not yet developed.		
Toddler: 1½ to 3 (Anal Phase)	Feels good when parent praises; feels bad when reprimanded. Enjoys being praised, admired; acts in ways to get praise, admiration. Self-feeling shifts back and forth between high and low, depending on others' evaluations. Few standards of his own. Frequent shifts in self-feelings and in confidence which is easily shaken.	Parent's praise or criticism has no effect; untouched by their opinions.	Focused on what parents will say. Most actions oriented toward getting their approval, avoiding their criticism.
Differentiating Stage: 3½ to 4 (Phallic Phase)	Proud of being a boy/girl; proud of body, appearance, capabilities. Feels lovable, good, worthwhile, attractive, competent. Expects to be liked by others. Positive feelings about self when "good" or acts appropriately; negative feelings when "bad" or acts inappropriately. Most of the time appears to have a good opinion of self. (Girls more likely than boys to have self-feelings influenced by others' evaluations and by the situation.)	Ashamed of being a boy/girl or of his/her body, appearance, capabilities. Feels unlovable, bad, worthless, hateful, unattractive, inadequate, incompetent. Expects not to be liked by others. Appears to have low self-esteem. Opinion of self is not good. "Inferiority feelings."	Appears grandiose, as overcompensation for low self-esteem. Acts superior — to cover up. May show extreme shifts back and forth between very high and very low self-esteem, depending on others' evaluations and on the situation.

Phase	Characteristic, expected, typical	Uncharacteristic, unexpected, atypical, pathological	
		Ranging from:	To:
Family Integration: $4\frac{1}{2}$ to 6 (Oedipal Phase)	Achieves own standards and sees self as successful. Appears to feel self-confident, self-assured; secure about his abilities; competent. Usually proud of his own work; takes pride in doing things well. Wants to emulate ideal of parents. Idealizes and identifies with parents and wants to comply with their demands.	Usually sets standards unrealistically high. Cannot meet own standards and sees self as unsuccessful. Feels inadequate in meeting own standards, feels stupid, bad. Appears to lack self-confidence; feels insecure about own abilities; doubts self. Usually not proud of own work.	Precociously identified with parental values; acts like "small adult." Perfectionistic. Righteous about own behavior. Intolerant with others. May appear smug.

Chapter 8
Assessment of
Developmental Progression

Though each of the five aspects of development—social, emotional, ego, phase, and superego—can be considered and assessed separately, and each certainly has a significant contribution to make to the overall assessment of the developmental progression of a child, the final assessment is not simply a summing up of the five. Rather it resembles an organic integration, where the final outcome is more than the sum of the parts.

Such an assessment, with the emphasis on a global impression of the child's development, allows a differentiation between (1) children who are progressing in their development and those who have some interference in their development and (2) children who show minimal pathology and those whose pathology is significant to the extent that it slows or temporarily interrupts further development.

Variations in Development

The task of assessing developmental progression is complicated by the fact that there are many variations in development. We find children who show overlapping phases of development, rather than neatly separated phases. For example, with some children, there were manifestations of the oral, anal, and phallic phases during the oedipal phase of development.

Although some children showed little fluctuation of progressive and regressive movement, others showed so much fluctuation of progression and regression that even experienced clinicians had difficulty deciding the significance to place on the fixations or regressive manifestations at a given time. Thus, it appears that for some children development moves forward with only rare regression, while for others there is an ease of regression and almost a fluidity of developmental movement.

In addition to the preceding variations, we found some children with an evenness of development in all areas, whereas others experienced unevenness, with precocity in some aspects, such as language or interpersonal relations. Furthermore, each child appears to follow his own timetable of progression, and this has to be taken into consideration in assessing his development. For some, development may proceed in slow motion for a while and then spurt forward, while for others the opposite pattern occurs. Some show a slow steady rate of development throughout childhood, while others progress rapidly.

Thus, in assessing a given child, it is essential to become familiar with his unique pattern of development.

Meaning of Symptoms

Another complication in the task of assessing developmental progression is the fact that similar overt behavior may have different meanings for different children and that any one variable may be merely suggestive of the course of developmental progression. Disorders may be related more to one phase of development than to another. Or, the same symptom may be overdetermined; a behavior can look oral and yet have a meaning on the anal, phallic, or oedipal level. For instance, a child may give evidence of separation anxiety, and the fear of leaving a parent or care-taking person may have different meanings, which cannot be detected by observation alone. The child may be afraid of the mother's leaving because of his own wishes against her, and, out of guilt, he may therefore need to cling to her. Or, he may have fears of loss and of losing the love of the parent; he may fear that his behavior will turn the parent away from him. Thus, the child may be afraid that the parent will not be available to depend on when he needs her or him. These are expressions of different levels of development which may be expressed by the symptom of separation anxiety.

In view of the factors just discussed, it would be important for those studying a given child to investigate the symptoms more closely to determine the level of psychic organization. This is particularly significant in order to decide the need for treatment. Since any specific behavior can represent an intermixture of drive, ego, and superego components, it must therefore be assessed in terms of each aspect of development.

There may be symptoms transitional in nature, which are appropriate for a specific phase of development. Such symptoms may reach great intensity in some children, while in others there may be only a comparatively mild expression of them. Phase-appropriate symptoms—as an expression of an internal struggle which is part of the organization and reorganization during the ever-changing development of the child—need not imply abnormal development. For example, there are the negativistic expressions of the child during the training period, or the insistence on rituals and little tolerance for changes. Or, there are the nightmares and the fears of the five- and six-year olds, which at times can be quite intense. These are signs (and at times symptoms) that are part of the phase conflicts through which the child passes, and we assume that at the appropriate time a new psychic organization will overcome these conflicts.

Some symptoms occur and eventually disappear without affecting development, and new symptoms appear. Often fears may disappear, and obsessive symptoms may appear instead.

Symptoms may shift from one content to another, while the underlying problem may still be the same. The change in itself, or the disappearance of one symptom, may not mean the underlying difficulties have been resolved but rather that the newly emerging symptoms of the child may be the new way in which the old conflicts emerge during the new phase of development.

Today, deviations and pathologies find a broader expression than in specific isolated symptoms. There are characterological deviations or personality attitudes which are inappropriate, and these may be expressed as a sense of inadequacy, low self-esteem, or inappropriate guilt.

Prevalence of Pathology

In the extensive and comprehensive longitudinal study of nonclinical children (a select group of "normal" children considered by their parents and teachers to be functioning more or less adequately at home and in the nursery-school situation), it was found that *every* child at some time had some behaviors or symptoms that might be considered pathological. The fundamental question, therefore, was, How much of the child's development had been affected by the pathology? If the child was still able to function adequately and to progress in significant areas, would this indicate that the symptom or problem was not taking up so much of the child's energies and so impairing his functioning that it interfered with developmental progression? Any symptom, conflict, pathology, or disorder had to be examined within the context of the total picture.

It is of significance to the adults assessing the child whether the child's difficulties are a response to a new or acute situation and therefore only reactive or whether they have become part of the child's functioning. Certain symptoms are a temporary adaptive response to a stressful situation and would be expected to disappear under different circumstances. Other symptoms, more internalized by the child, may show continuity over many different situations.

Pathology may or may not interfere with developmental progression. Even if it does interfere, later developmental progression may overcome the interference. Development may be interfered with for a short or long period of time and then be resumed. A child may need a shorter or longer time to recover from events such as the beginning of nursery school, the illness or death of a parent, the birth of a sibling, the divorce or separation of parents, or moving to a new city. Such stress situations may lead to pathology and/or interference with development. The interference may have occurred earlier and may have continued into subsequent phases, or it may be limited to the current phase of the child's development.

Thus, in assessing a child, there are two separate but major considerations: (1) whether or not there is pathology and (2) whether development has been interfered with in significant areas or is continuing.

Recommendations

Once a judgment has been made that there is pathology in significant areas, or that there is interference with development, the next step is to explore possible explanations for this finding and then to make recommendations for action. For example, is the observed behavior or symptom the child's reaction to a recent or current change in his situation, or is it part of a long-continuing constellation? The answer to such a question is of assistance to the teacher, child-care worker, community-health professional, pediatrician, or whoever is assessing the child, in considering various types of action to take with this child and formulating recommendations for specific action.

Some problems can be approached by recommending changes in the relationship of the adult and environment to the child, as for example, by giving the child more individual attention or by arranging for him to engage in certain special activities.

Teachers oriented toward the development of children often will outline a curriculum for the group according to the age of the children and within the group will take cognizance of the individual development of each child and the appropriateness of his developmental behavior in making recommendations for further action.

On the other hand, there may be situations in which a child cannot function appropriately in a specific environment, and the recommendation may be in terms of removing the child from the school-group that precipitated or accentuated his problems and placing him in a new group where he may try out different and novel ways of interacting with his peers.

Other problems may be dealt with by recommending a meeting with the child's parents to discuss the situation with them and to give them an awareness of the difficulties the child is having and some indication as to how he could be helped at home or how the stresses on the child could be lessened or minimized. Having such awareness, parents usually are creative in trying to find ways and means to lead the child to a resolution of conflicts or to a new sense of achievement or coping mechanisms which are appropriate for his age and the demands of the situation.

The most serious problems may be dealt with by recommending a consultation with a mental health specialist who could offer advice or who might suggest a more intensive clinical study of the child or therapeutic help.

Thus, by determining that a child's development is not progressing as expected, and by reviewing the child's strengths and weaknesses, as well as his current situation, recommended plans for actions can be more realistically based. During the nursery school-kindergarten period, the interplay between parents, teachers, pediatricians, social workers, and other caretaking personnel is very important so as to achieve a concerted effort in which the interests of the child are understood and modalities are outlined, which are coordinated for the benefit of the child.

Physical Health

Physical health is included in the *Assessment Outline of Early Child Development* to prevent one-sided decisions about emotional problems. Because the state of a child's physical health can affect progression in social, emotional, and ego development, it is important to know if a child is physically healthy, if he has chronic physical problems or frequent illnesses, if he is often hospitalized, or if he has significant physical impairment.

Similarly, disturbances in developmental progression may be reflected in physical health. Physical dysfunctioning or somatization and psychosomatic symptoms or conversion reactions may be an expression of conflict; there may be allergies, asthma, headaches, stomach aches, frequent colds, frequent accidents, etc. Thus, it is advisable that, when it seems appropriate, a physical examination be recommended in addition to educational and developmental recommendations.

Uses of Short Assessment Outline

The *Assessment Outline of Early Child Development* is designed to be used by nursery-school and kindergarten teachers, day-care and community-health workers, physicians, psychiatrists, psychologists, social workers, nurses, family-life educators, and others who care for young children.

The outline is intended to be used flexibly. It is designed to alert adults to the developmental state of a child and to some of the child's problem areas and can assist in making explicit what is known about the child. It is not intended to be used as a substitute for a detailed clinical report about a child's functioning but only as an initial screening procedure, suggesting directions for further action. Through its use, children who need special attention or further intensive study can be identified, and if necessary clinicians can then be brought in either for consultation or for a more complete assessment.

The *Assessment Outline of Early Child Development* regularly used will permit comparisons of a child at different times. By filling it out at the beginning and at the end of the year, it is possible to determine whether a child is showing continuing progression in development or some interference and to see in which areas of development changes have taken place.

Teachers may choose to use it only at the beginning of a semester as a basis for planning a program for the child's activities or only at the end of the year as a summary statement about the child, to be used by others who will have contact with him in the future.

In our work with educational and training institutions, we found that the *Assessment Outline of Early Child Development* was often useful as a teaching device in college undergraduate or graduate courses concered with child development or for in-service training programs with professionals and paraprofessionals. It provided these individuals with new information about early child development and with a different approach in looking at children. For some, the outline itself suggested ways in which a nonclinician could have a role in modifying the child's environment.

Clinical and nonclinical persons who are asked to make judgments about the various aspects of development must observe children more closely than they usually have. As a consequence, they may achieve a new orientation and a sharpened perception that will enable them to note behaviors they previously had not noticed. In addition, they may begin to recognize hitherto overlooked problems of the child or may become aware of some of the ways the young child interacts with his environment. This, in turn, may affect the adult's own interactions with the child and guide him in future planning for the child.

It has been recognized for a long time that at this early age the child's environment is of great importance to his development and that the parents because of their early and continuing influence on the child are the primary figures in this environment. They can support or fail to support ego strength; they can act as models for identification; they can reinforce regressive moves; they can overgratify certain drives. Therefore, another suggested use of the *Assessment Outline of Early Child Development* is as a basis for conferences with parents—to indicate the problem areas of the child in his developmental progression and possibly to point out to them some of the effects of their behaviors on the child.

Chapter 9
Assessment Outline of
Early Child Development

The *Assessment Outline of Early Child Development* is designed as a guide to help formulate and make explicit what one knows about a given child. It permits the study of the child's progression or lack of progression in development and points out the specific factors that are important in his development. It does not lead to a clinical diagnostic statement, but it can be used as an adjunct by providing the developmental components of the child's deviation.

The *Assessment Outline of Early Child Development* is to be filled out on the basis of one's direct experience with the child rather than on the basis of information received about the child from other sources. It can be filled out after even a brief period of contact with a child. As with any guide, however, it is unlikely that *all* the information that one desires about a specific child will be included. To enhance its usefulness we suggest that, for one's own purposes, one may want to reformulate a statement or add statements that are not included in the *Assessment Outline of Early Child Development*.

Based on one's responses to the items in the first part of the *Assessment Outline of Early Child Development*, as well as on comments one has made in the provided spaces, one can proceed, in

Mr. Ruediger Schroeer helped in devising this version of the *Assessment Outline of Early Child Development* and in determining its validity and reliability.

the second part, to make a final assessment of the child and to indicate the problems the child has; and this, in turn, will lead to recommendations for correcting these problems.

The *Assessment Outline of Early Child Development* usually requires twenty to thirty minutes to fill out (though the first time may require a few minutes longer). This outline is not intended to be used as a substitute for a longer, more intensive report but as an initial assessment, suggesting directions for action. We found it to be helpful to have the *Assessment Outline of Early Child Development* used at various times during the year in order to evaluate changes. It may also serve as a year-end summary or as a report to others or as a means for conferring with the child's parents.

Longitudinal assessments are also important in order to see in which areas changes occur over a period of time and whether these changes occur toward progression in development or toward pathology and interference with development. Sometimes it is not easy to assess the changes which occur within a short period of time. It may be difficult to determine whether new problems are emerging or whether these are replacing the old ones or whether a new organization is occurring. Only the year-by-year continuous assessment can give evidence about the general developmental progression of the child.

IDENTIFYING DATA

Child's Name _____ Date _____

Birth date _____ Sex _____ Birth Position _____ Number of Siblings _____

Birthdate of Father _____ Birthdate of Mother _____

Education of Father _____ Education of Mother _____

Occupation of Father _____ Occupation of Mother _____

Date Child Entered School _____ Date Child Entered Present Group _____

Previous Schooling on Group Experience:

Previous Test Records:

Other Pertinent Information About the Child:

Directions for the Next Page

On the next page you will find nine items that deal with the development of various abilities. Indicate how this child compares with other children the same age by circling the appropriate number.

Circling (1) indicates that on the given item this child seems like children *much younger* than his chronological age.

Circling (2) indicates that on the given item this child seems like children *somewhat younger* than his chronological age.

Circling (3) indicates that on the given item this child seems about *average* for his chronological age.
Circling (4) indicates that on the given item this child seems *above average* for his chronological age.

In addition, in order to individualize your assessment of this child, in the column on the right you may record:

    (a) recent changes
    (b) conditions under which the ability varies
    (c) how the ability is manifested
    (d) any other comments

Hypothetical example:

Item	Comparison with others the same chronological age	Recent changes, conditions under which the ability varies, how the ability is manifested, any other comments
Ability to deal with difficult or new situations	1 ② 3 4	Has recently become worse. Handles some new situations adequately, but often withdraws or retreats inappropriately when a stranger comes into the room.

In this hypothetical example, the respondent has indicated that this child's ability to deal with difficult or new situations is below average compared to other children the same age, and that this ability has recently lessened.

Item	Comparison with others the same chronological age	Recent changes, conditions under which the ability varies, how the ability is manifested, any other comments
Coordination of large body movement	1 2 3 4	
Coordination of small body movement (dexterity)	1 2 3 4	
Vocabulary	1 2 3 4	
Verbal communication with adults	1 2 3 4	
Verbal communication with children	1 2 3 4	
Ability to use various materials	1 2 3 4	
Ability to deal with difficult or new situations	1 2 3 4	
Ability to wait and/or take turns	1 2 3 4	
Ability to pay attention and to concentrate	1 2 3 4	
Curiosity, interest in exploring and learning	1 2 3 4	

(1) Like children much younger than his chronological age
(2) Like children somewhat younger than his chronological age
(3) About average for his chronological age
(4) Above average for chronological age

Directions for the Next Two Pages

On the next two pages you will find items that deal with affection, aggression, and mood, as well as items that are labeled "miscellaneous." Indicate how often the child shows the various qualities of behaviors or emotions by circling the appropriate number for each.

Indicate that this child shows the particular quality of behavior or emotion by circling

(0) Not at all   (1) Rarely   (2) Some of the time   (3) Most of the time

(If you cannot respond to a specific item, leave it blank until you have further information. Often there is not enough information available about the child's interaction with a parent, and it is only after a period of sensitive observation that the item can be marked.)

In addition, in order to individualize your assessment of this child, in the column on the right you may record:

(a) recent changes
(b) circumstances that stimulate the specific quality of behavior and/or emotion
(c) whether emotions felt are directly expressed or are covered up
(d) how the feelings are expressed
(e) any other comments

Hypothetical example:

Item	Qualities of Behaviors or Emotions				Recent changes, circumstances that stimulate the specific quality of behavior and/or emotion, whether emotions felt are directly expressed or are covered up, how the feelings are expressed, any other comments
Expression of affection with	extreme, intense	artificial, exaggerated, overdemonstrative	very controlled or inhibited	open, direct spontaneous	
mother	⓪1 2 3	⓪1 2 3	0 1 2 ③	⓪1 2 3	This has been a problem of long standing. Once in a while he may briefly hold another child's hand.
father	⓪1 2 3	⓪1 2 3	0 1 2 ③	⓪1 2 3	
teacher	⓪1 2 3	⓪1 2 3	0 1 ② ③	⓪1 2 3	
children	0 1 2 3	⓪1 2 3	0 1 2 ③	0 1 ② 3	

In this hypothetical example, the respondent has indicated that most of the time this child is very controlled or inhibited in his expression of affection with mother, father, teacher, and children. Sometimes the child can spontaneously express affection with children. This is a probleem of long standing.

Item	Qualities of Behaviors or Emotions				Recent changes, circumstances which stimulate the specific quality of behavior and/or emotion, whether emotions felt are directly expressed or are covered up, how the feelings are expressed, any other comments.
Expression of affection with	extreme, intense	artificial, exaggerated, overdemonstrative	very controlled or inhibited	open, direct spontaneous	
mother	0 1 2 3	0 1 2 3	0 1 2 3	0 1 2 3	
father	0 1 2 3	0 1 2 3	0 1 2 3	0 1 2 3	
teacher	0 1 2 3	0 1 2 3	0 1 2 3	0 1 2 3	
children	0 1 2 3	0 1 2 3	0 1 2 3	0 1 2 3	
Response to expression of affection from	shows strong need for it	anxious, uncomfortable	ignores, acts uninterested	accepts easily, pleased, responsive	
mother	0 1 2 3	0 1 2 3	0 1 2 3	0 1 2 3	
father	0 1 2 3	0 1 2 3	0 1 2 3	0 1 2 3	
teacher	0 1 2 3	0 1 2 3	0 1 2 3	0 1 2 3	
children	0 1 2 3	0 1 2 3	0 1 2 3	0 1 2 3	
Expression of aggression toward	extreme, intense	artificial, exaggerated, caricatured	very controlled or inhibited	moderate, direct, spontaneous	
mother	0 1 2 3	0 1 2 3	0 1 2 3	0 1 2 3	
father	0 1 2 3	0 1 2 3	0 1 2 3	0 1 2 3	
teacher	0 1 2 3	0 1 2 3	0 1 2 3	0 1 2 3	
children	0 1 2 3	0 1 2 3	0 1 2 3	0 1 2 3	
Response to reprimands of	extreme aggression	anxiety, withdrawal	seems to ignore, not notice	tolerates, responds moderately	
mother	0 1 2 3	0 1 2 3	0 1 2 3	0 1 2 3	
father	0 1 2 3	0 1 2 3	0 1 2 3	0 1 2 3	
teacher	0 1 2 3	0 1 2 3	0 1 2 3	0 1 2 3	

(0) Not at all
(1) Rarely
(2) Some of the time
(3) Most of the time

Qualities of Behaviors or Emotions

Item					Recent changes, circumstances which stimulate the specific quality of beahavior and/or emotion, whether emotions felt are directly expressed or are covered up, how the feelings are expressed, any other comments
Response to expression of aggression by children	extreme aggression 0 1 2 3	anxiety, withdrawal 0 1 2 3	seems to ignore, not notice 0 1 2 3	tolerates, responds moderately 0 1 2 3	
Characteristic mood	angry, annoyed 0 1 2 3	anxious, fearful 0 1 2 3	sad, unhappy 0 1 2 3	happy, contented 0 1 2 3	

Miscellaneous

Characteristic Descriptions

Item					Recent changes, circumstances that stimulate the specific behavior, any other comments
Body activity	rigid, stiff 0 1 2 3	slow, cautious 0 1 2 3	wild and/or uncontrolled 0 1 2 3	free and spontaneous 0 1 2 3	
Social interaction	alone 0 1 2 3	with teacher 0 1 2 3	with one child 0 1 2 3	with group of children 0 1 2 3	
Quality of play	solitary 0 1 2 3	parallel and/or imitative 0 1 2 3	competitive, challenging 0 1 2 3	cooperative 0 1 2 3	

(0) Not at all   (2) Some of the time
(1) Rarely   (3) Most of the time

Directions for the Next Three Pages

On the next three pages you will find items that outline developmental characteristics and social relationships. Indicate how often the child shows the characteristic or behavior by circling the appropriate number for each.

Circling (0) indicates that the characteristic or behavior is observed *not at all.*
Circling (1) indicates that the characteristic or behavior is observed *rarely.*
Circling (2) indicates that the characteristic or behavior is observed *some of the time.*
Circling (3) indicates that the characteristic or behavior is observed *most of the time.*

(If you cannot respond to a specific item, leave it blank until you have further information. Often there is not enough information available about the child's interaction with a parent; and it is only after a period of sensitive observation that the item can be marked.)

In addition, in order to individualize your assessment of this child, in the column on the right you may record:

(a) recent changes
(b) circumstances which stimulate the characteristic or behavior
(c) how the characteristic or behavior is shown
(d) a phrase that better describes the child
(e) any other comments

Hypothetical example:

Characteristic	Father	Mother	Teacher	Boys	Girls	Recent changes, circumstances that stimulate the characteristic or behavior, how the characteristic or behavior is shown, a phrase that better describes the child, any other comments.
Complains to, whines when with	0 1 2 ③	0 1 2 ③	0 1 2 ③	0 ① 2 3	0 1 ② 3	Complains to parents about what other children have that he does not have; to teacher that other children have wronged him; to girls when he feels they are not playing fair. Less complaining recently.

In this hypothetical example, the respondent has indicated that most of the complaining is to adults and some is to girls; but there is rarely any complaining to boys. There has been improvement recently.

Characteristic	Father	Mother	Teacher	Boys	Girls	Recent changes, circumstances which stimulate the characteristic or behavior, how the characteristic or behavior is shown, a phrase that better describes the child, any other comments.
Obedient, compliant with	0 1 2 3	0 1 2 3	0 1 2 3	0 1 2 3	0 1 2 3	
Clings to	0 1 2 3	0 1 2 3	0 1 2 3	0 1 2 3	0 1 2 3	
Apathetic, withdrawn with	0 1 2 3	0 1 2 3	0 1 2 3	0 1 2 3	0 1 2 3	
Dependent on	0 1 2 3	0 1 2 3	0 1 2 3	0 1 2 3	0 1 2 3	
Demanding with	0 1 2 3	0 1 2 3	0 1 2 3	0 1 2 3	0 1 2 3	
Complains to, whines when with	0 1 2 3	0 1 2 3	0 1 2 3	0 1 2 3	0 1 2 3	
Asks for help from	0 1 2 3	0 1 2 3	0 1 2 3	0 1 2 3	0 1 2 3	
Negative, defiant to	0 1 2 3	0 1 2 3	0 1 2 3	0 1 2 3	0 1 2 3	
Stubborn toward	0 1 2 3	0 1 2 3	0 1 2 3	0 1 2 3	0 1 2 3	
Bossy, domineering with	0 1 2 3	0 1 2 3	0 1 2 3	0 1 2 3	0 1 2 3	

(0) Not at all
(1) Rarely
(2) Some of the time
(3) Most of the time

Characteristic	Father	Mother	Teacher	Boys	Girls	Recent changes, circumstances which stimulate the characteristic or behavior, how the characteristic or behavior is shown, a phrase that better describes the child, any other comments.
Friendly, cooperative with	0 1 2 3	0 1 2 3	0 1 2 3	0 1 2 3	0 1 2 3	
Competitive, bragging, challenging with	0 1 2 3	0 1 2 3	0 1 2 3	0 1 2 3	0 1 2 3	
Assertive, forceful with	0 1 2 3	0 1 2 3	0 1 2 3	0 1 2 3	0 1 2 3	
Passive, unassertive with	0 1 2 3	0 1 2 3	0 1 2 3	0 1 2 3	0 1 2 3	
Actively seeks attention of	0 1 2 3	0 1 2 3	0 1 2 3	0 1 2 3	0 1 2 3	
Avoids attention of	0 1 2 3	0 1 2 3	0 1 2 3	0 1 2 3	0 1 2 3	
Shows off to	0 1 2 3	0 1 2 3	0 1 2 3	0 1 2 3	0 1 2 3	
Seductive, manipulating with	0 1 2 3	0 1 2 3	0 1 2 3	0 1 2 3	0 1 2 3	
Shows concern and sympathy for	0 1 2 3	0 1 2 3	0 1 2 3	0 1 2 3	0 1 2 3	
Aware of and responsive to the needs and feelings of	0 1 2 3	0 1 2 3	0 1 2 3	0 1 2 3	0 1 2 3	

(0) Not at all
(1) Rarely
(2) Some of the time
(3) Most of the time

Characteristic	Frequency	Recent changes, circumstances which stimulate the characteristic or behavior, how the characteristic or behavior is shown, a phrase that better describes the child, any other comments.
Gets hurt by other children	0 1 2 3	
Hurts other children	0 1 2 3	
Hurts self	0 1 2 3	
Is organized, orderly	0 1 2 3	
Is disorganized, disorderly	0 1 2 3	
Admires self, proud of self	0 1 2 3	
Admires others	0 1 2 3	
Criticizes self, finds fault with self	0 1 2 3	
Criticizes others, finds fault with others	0 1 2 3	
Expresses or shows guilt; anticipates punishment	0 1 2 3	

(0) Not at all   (2) Some of the time
(1) Rarely   (3) Most of the time

HEALTH

Check those boxes and answer the questions that apply to this child

| *General Health:* | Poor | Fair | Good | Excellent | Describe any problems: |

| *Hearing:* | Poor | Fair | Good | Describe any problems: |
| | Not checked within last six months | Checked within last six months | |

| | Poor | Fair | Good | Describe any problems: |
| | Not checked within last six months | Checked within last six months | |

| *Speech Impediments:* | Yes, and interfere with communication | Yes, but do not interfere with communication | NO | Describe speech impediments: |

| *Other Handicaps:* | Yes, and interfere with functioning | Yes, but do not interfere with functioning | NO | Describe handicaps: |

Does this child have any symptoms or difficulties that you consider to be significant? (e.g. spitting, biting, excessive thumb-sucking, eating difficulties, inappropriate fears for his age, difficulties in toilet training, excessive daydreaming, separation difficulties, etc.) Yes _____ No _____ Describe the symptoms or difficulties:

Your concerns about this child:
(You may include here reference to the child's family or life situation, as well as the development of the child.)

Strengths of this child:
(You may want to include the child's intelligence, learning capacity, adaptive functioning or other aspects of his personality which are not covered in this Assessment Outline but which you consider significant.)

Specific areas which need further investigation and clarification:

A. Final Assessment

Circle either 1, 2, 3, or 4 to indicate which best expresses your opinion.

(It may be difficult to decide whether to put a child into group 2 or group 3, and this in itself is an important statement.)

1. *This child is able to progress developmentally.*
   He is within the expected range for his age and sex. His functioning would be considered age adequate. No special help or attention is necessary.

2. *This child is progressing developmentally though he has problems in some areas.*
   He has conflicts and difficulties which are beyond the norm. (Certain symptoms occur in response to the environment and are not as significant as other symptoms. Therefore, any symptom is to be looked at within the total picture of developmental progression.)

3. *This child's development is not progressing appropriately.*
   There are problems that interfere with development in significant areas. (Such problems might include still depending on mother and being unable to move away from her toward other people; showing hyperactivity or impulsivity without appropriate controls; having serious learning difficulties; showing difficulty in expressing feelings; etc.)

4. *This child had problems that had interfered with his developmental progression but is currently showing improvement.*
   This is based on a recent change in the child in the direction of overcoming a symptom or coping with problems. It includes even children who are slowly starting to change; it is the change that is significant. The child might be recovering from a traumatic event, such as the illness of a parent, the birth of a sibling, change of residence, etc. Because of the trauma, there may have been some inhibition or regression before the development began moving forward again.

B. *Possible Explanations for 2, 3, or 4.*
Of the following explanations, circle as many numbers as you feel are necessary; and if you circle #1, underline all the phrases which you think are possibilities.

1. *These problems are probably a reaction to a recent or current situation.*

   e.g., Starting nursery-school, a separation of parents, death of a significant person, illness of a family member or other significant person, birth of a sibling, change of residency, trip.
   Other _____

2. *These problems are probably a direct consequence of the particular group the child is in at school.*

3. *These problems are part of the child's general behavior pattern.*

4. These problems are due to _____

C. *Recommendations for action.*
Circle as many numbers as necessary.

1. *Helping within the educational setting.* Providing special consideration for the child, such as the teacher giving him more individual time, arranging for him to engage in special activities, providing more opportunities for contact with specific other children, assisting in impulse control, assisting in developing motor skills, assisting in the separation process, or in other ways providing a corrective experience within the educational setting.

2. *Parental guidance.* Discussing the child's problems with the parent(s) in the hope that by giving the parent(s) an awareness of the child's difficulties, the parent(s) would then be able to act in a way to help the child or to minimize the problems. Specific goals with parents _____

3. *Changing the educational setting.* Putting the child into a different group at school in the hope that moving him from a group that precipitated or accentuated the problem would in itself be therapeutic.

4. *Consulting with a mental health professional* to discuss and evaluate the child's behavior.

5. *Referring the child to a mental health resource for treatment.*

6. *Deciding that no special action is necessary* in the expectation that the problem is transitory and will disappear in the natural course of development.

7. *Other* (e.g., physical check-up, speech therapy, dance therapy, art therapy, special attention to physical handicaps, etc.)

CONTINUOUS RECORD

Date	Grouping of Child (Group 1, 2, 3, 4)	Items or areas that have not changed and continue to be significant	Items or areas that have changed

Appendix A
Reduction to the
Essential Features

The items in the short version of the *Assessment Outline of Early Child Development* are the result of three different analyses of the data gathered in our research. First, the research staff undertook an intensive content analysis of the dynamic summaries that had been written by the clinicians. The purpose of the analysis was to determine which aspects of development, as well as which specific behaviors or characteristics within each area, were mentioned as a basis for assessing a given child. From such a content analysis, it was possible to discover those aspects or behaviors the clinicians indicated as being important for their final judgments in evaluating the children.

Second, an extensive outline of items of behavior and aspects of development was prepared, based on the recorded interviews with parents, teachers, and children and on the observations of the children in the school setting. For each child, the clinician who had been the interviewer and observer evaluated each of the items on a five-point scale according to the significance it had to him in arriving at his final assessment. Despite individual differences among the clinicians in their responses, certain items were regarded by all clinicians as more significant than others.

Third, research staff members who had not studied the children were given a comprehensive outline of behaviors and aspects of development. These members completed the outline for each child based on the recorded interviews and observations and then made a judgment about the child's grouping. This procedure showed what information could be obtained from the interviews and observations and also which items were specific for different groupings of children.

Following these three types of analyses, the items which were not relevant for the groupings of the children were eliminated from the final short version of the *Assessment Outline of Early Child Development*. Also omitted from the final outline were items which the clinicians indicated were of little or no significance in making an assessment of the child's developmental progression.

In addition, items were eliminated for which there was insufficient information from the interviews or the observations to make a judgment for many of the children. For example, it was considered desirable to judge the child's capacity to differentiate between fantasy and reality. But when questions were asked of the parents and teachers about the child's fantasies, they could not give answers to provide the necessary information. This information was more available and more easily evaluated from the psychological tests.

Criteria for Outline

Several criteria were specifically set forth in advance as guidelines for the final version of the *Assessment Outline of Early Child Development*. One criterion was that only those aspects of development found by the investigation to be *most significant as indicators* of developmental progression and/or pathology were to be included. The assessment of the nonclinical children in the research study had been a much more sophisticated and extensive process than was necessary or useful for a short assessment. However, from such an extensive and intensive investigation, it was possible, as already described, to determine what was important in order for nonclinicians to differentiate between children who showed developmental progression and children who showed interference with development in significant areas, and also to become aware of children with pathology.

Another criterion was that the short version of the *Assessment Outline of Early Child Development* was to be limited to the *minimum material necessary.* Since only a gross assessment of a young child's development was to be made, it was preferable to include only the items essential for this purpose. The goal was to develop an outline that could be completed in twenty to thirty minutes—a significant reduction from the twenty-five hours that had been required for a complete clinical workup and assessment of each child.

A third criterion was that there was to be *concentration on those aspects of development and items of behavior most accessible to non-clinicians and most useful to them* in their direct contacts with young children. This meant including the behaviors usually mentioned by teachers and parents in their interviews and eliminating items that required inferential reasoning or interpretation by clinicians.

Finally, it was decided that all items were to be *stated in a simple, unambiguous, and direct way and in language relevant to those* who would ultimately be using this short version of the *Assessment Outline of Early Child Development.*

Format for Outline

Various formats were tried before arriving at the final *Assessment Outline of Early Child Development.* The first format used open-ended questions similar to those used for the interviews with parents and teachers. However, nonclinical professionals who filled these out objected that the task was tedious and took too long. When a format was tried in which only multiple choice items were presented, the respondents objected that this did not do justice to some children because they had to "squeeze" children into the alternatives presented.

Therefore, the final format presents a rating system for the various items along with space for comments about the individual child and instructions that encourage the respondents to mark the outline flexibly, keeping in mind how the respondent plans to use the results of the assessment.

Preliminary Trials

The *Assessment Outline of Early Child Development* was first tried out with teachers who had been participating in the ongoing research projects. They had been interviewed by the staff clinicians and were acquainted with the information being sought about the children under study.

Then, the *Assessment Outline* was used by a group of teachers in the pre-kindergarten group in the New York City public school system and by some of the teachers in the therapeutic nursery school at the Child Development Center.

All of the teachers who participated in the testing assisted the project by criticizing the various formats, correcting the language and emphasizing the need to simplify the wording, offering phrases for the rating scales, and even suggesting the use of different colored paper for different sections of the *Assessment Outline of Early Child Development.*

Appendix B
Validity and Reliability

Since the item selection for the *Assessment Outline of Early Child Development* was based on the theoretical assumptions of the study, this assured that the information gathered would also be within the same theoretical framework and thus provided content validity. However, in order to make sure that, as a result of the many changes in format and in the wording of items, information was not lost and that the final version did not bias assessment, other analyses were carried out.

When comparisons of the different assessments were made, three types of agreement were distinguished:

1. Agreement about Developmental Progression. The groupings by nonclinicians and the groupings by clinicians agreed that developmental progression had or had not been maintained. That is, both believed that the given child belonged in either Group 1a (progression in development had been maintained as would be expected) or Group 1b (progression in development had been maintained but with significant accompanying pathological features).

2. Agreement about Pathology. The groupings by nonclinicians and the groupings by clinicians agreed that pathology existed. That is, both believed that the given child belonged in either Group 1b (progression in development has been maintained, but with significant accompanying pathological features) or Group 2 (development has been interfered with in significant areas).

3. Complete Agreement. The groupings by nonclinicians and the groupings by clinicians agreed that developmental progression had or had not been maintained *and* agreed that significant pathology did or did not occur. That is, both believed that the given child belonged in the same group.

In our study, when we compared the overall assessments based on an integration of all information by the clinicians with the assessments based on *only* the teacher interviews, there was 72 percent agreement for the boys and 71 percent agreement for the girls. Thus, the information from the teacher interviews alone could give a fairly accurate preliminary assessment of the child's developmental progression.

The evaluations of the children made by teachers who filled out the *Assessment Outline of Early Child Development* were then compared with the evaluations of the children made by clinicians who integrated all the information from all sources—interviews with parents, teachers, and children; observations of the children in the school setting; and psychological tests.

As to whether or not developmental progression had been maintained, teachers using the *Assessment Outline of Early Child Development* and clinicians using an integration of all information available agreed on 93 percent of the children; as to the presence of pathology, the teachers and clinicians agreed on 80 percent of the children. There was agreement on both developmental progression and significant pathology—that is, complete agreement—on 73 percent of the children. Thus, the agreement between the clinicians' integration of all information available and the teachers' use of the *Assessment Outline of Early Child Development* was as good as the agreement between assessments based on the clinicians' integration of all information available and assessments based on the clinical interviews with teachers.

For the second type of analysis, a group of clinicians who did *not* do the original interviewing and therefore were not familiar with the child, read the clinical interviews of the teachers and filled out the *Assessment Outline of Early Child Development* on the basis of the information in the recorded interview. Following this, another group of clinicians, who had neither conducted the interviews nor read the report of the clinical interviews, assessed the children on the basis of just reading the completed *Assessment Outline of Early Child Development* for each child. As to whether developmental progression had been maintained, clinicians who assessed the children by just studying the *Assessment Outline of Early Child Development* for each child and clinicians who assessed the children by using an integration of all information available agreed on 93 percent of the children; as to whether significant pathology was present, they agreed on 87 percent of the children. There was agreement on both developmental progression and significant pathology—that is, complete agreement—on 80 percent of the children.

We questioned how the information given by the *Assessment Outline of Early Child Development* compared with the specific information obtained in the interview and observational material. Therefore, we asked a group of clinicians who were not familiar with the children to use *only* the completed *Assessment Outline of Early Child Development* and to write short descriptive statements about each child based on this information alone. They were instructed to write these descriptive statements in a style similar to that used by clinicians in writing dynamic summaries. This could then be used to determine whether the items in the *Assessment Outline of Early Child Development* provide enough data to describe the children in statements similar to those customarily used in clinical write-ups of the interview and observational material.

The brief descriptions written by the clinicians who did the initial interviewing and wrote dynamic summaries of the material were compared with the brief descriptions written by the clinicians who had used only the responses on the *Assessment Outline of Early Child Development*. There were striking similarities in the content of these descriptions pertaining to the discussions of social development, emotional development, ego development, phase development, and superego development.

Thus, we concluded that the information given by the *Assessment Outline of Early Child Development* allows assessment comparable to the assessments made by clinicians on the basis of interview and observational materials. We also concluded that the specific information available in the responses to the *Assessment Outline of Early Child Development* can be a basis for descriptive statements about a child comparable to the statements that might be found in any dynamic summary of clinical interviews with the child, his parents, and his teachers.

Some differences, however, do appear in the content of the clinical interviews and the content of the *Assessment Outline of Early Child Development*. The teacher-interview-based descriptions of the child's social development are somewhat more detailed than are the descriptions in the *Assessment Outline of Early Child Development*. On the other hand, the *Assessment Outline of Early Child Development* emphasizes the developmental characteristics of a child more than the interview descriptions do.

Another difference is in the area of the psychic experiences of the child, such as his needs and motivations. These are discussed in more detail in the teacher-interview-based descriptions than in the *Assessment Outline of Early Child Development*. This difference may be attributable to the fact that the clinicians can probe more in the interviews and follow up any questions they have about a specific response of the teacher.

Finally, the impression of the clinicians as to the accuracy of the teacher's responses was usually mentioned in the interview-based descriptions, whereas this cannot be evaluated when the *Assessment Outline of Early Child Development* is used.

Index